THE GREAT GATSBY
ANTHOLOGY

THE GREAT GATSBY
ANTHOLOGY

Poetry & Prose Inspired By
F. Scott Fitzgerald's Novel

Edited by

Melanie Villines

SILVER BIRCH PRESS
LOS ANGELES, CALIFORNIA

© 2015, Silver Birch Press

ISBN-13: 978-0692427064

ISBN-10: 0692427066

EMAIL: silver@silverbirchpress.com

WEB: silverbirchpress.com

BLOG: silverbirchpress.wordpress.com

MAILING ADDRESS:
Silver Birch Press
P.O. Box 29458
Los Angeles, CA 90029

COVER ART: "Wings of Victory" by Erté (*Harper's*, March 1919).

INTERIOR ART: 1920s illustrations by George Barbier (1882-1932).

Once again, to Scott

FOREWORD
by Melanie Villines

Why do so many people call *The Great Gatsby* their favorite novel, and come back to this story again and again?

The events in the book take place in 1922, nearly a century from this writing (2015)—but, like all classic tales, the story is timeless. For readers, the book satisfies on multiple levels—as a love story, a cautionary tale of unbridled greed, a time capsule, as well as a study of class (upper, middle, lower, and under). Most of all, the book is revered and remembered for Fitzgerald's remarkable prose, most famously the opening lines of Chapter III: "There was music from my neighbor's house through the summer nights. In his blue gardens men and girls came and went like moths among the whisperings and the champagne and the stars."

Like all masterpieces, the whole is greater than the sum of its parts—and it's difficult to pinpoint just why this novel stands above most (or all) others. It's enrapturing, haunting, engaging, beautiful, and tragic—which all add up to the one word that perhaps can take in all of these attributes: sublime.

Writers are especially drawn to this novel—Haruki Murakami, for one, credits *The Great Gatsby* as the inspiration for his entire career (and he even translated the book into Japanese), while renowned crime novelist Ross Macdonald called Fitzgerald "my master."

Because *The Great Gatsby* holds such a special place in many writers' minds and hearts, Silver Birch Press decided to celebrate the 90th anniversary of the novel's 1925 publication by issuing a call for submission for poetry and prose inspired by the book. In all, over eighty authors contributed to this collection with a wide variety of offerings that pay homage to Fitzgerald's beloved novel.

Join us in raising a glass of champagne to F. Scott Fitzgerald and congratulating him on his enduring classic.

TABLE OF CONTENTS

"I have read it three times...it has interested and excited me more than any new novel I have seen, either English or American, for a number of years ...It seems to me to be the first step than American fiction has taken since Henry James."

T.S. ELIOT

BY WAY OF INTRODUCTION

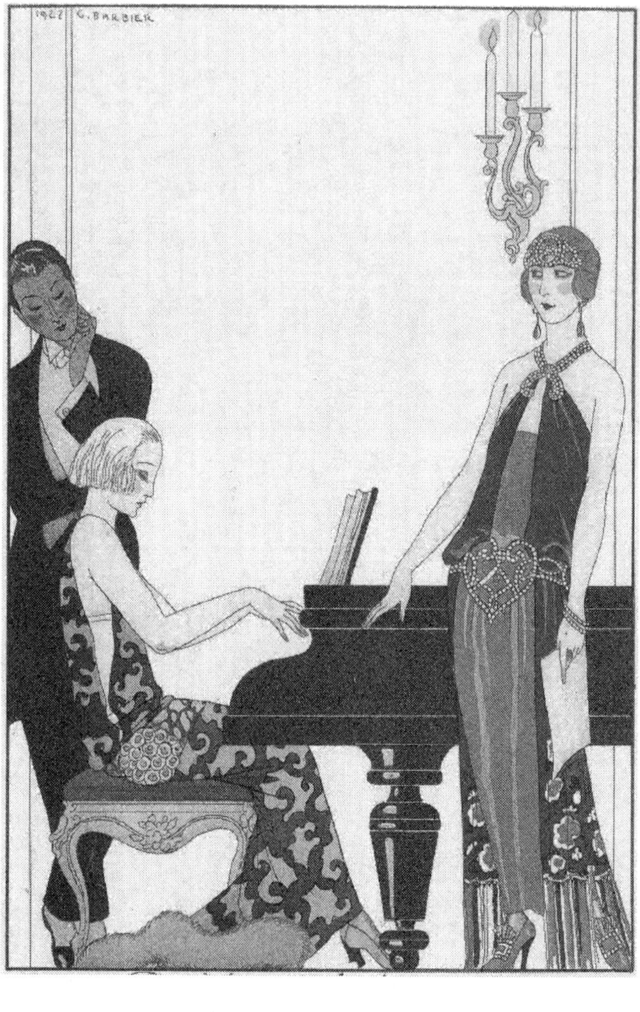

1922 G. BARBIER

slip it on
by Johannes S. H. Bjerg

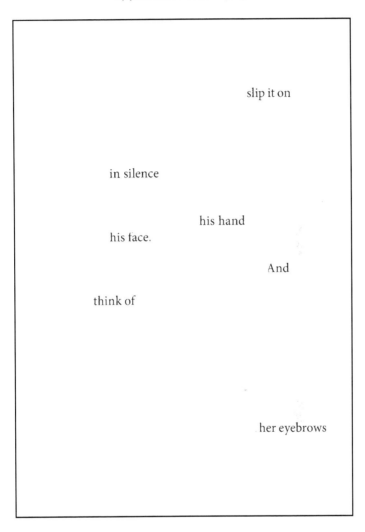

slip it on

in silence

his hand

his face.

And

think of

her eyebrows

Formality on Scalloped White Wings
by Samantha LeVan

the champagne is weeping
quavering soprano
singing dissention
about dignified struggle

the diamond, indifferent
occupied by reluctant promises
on scalloped white wings
curious only of stagnant notes

and the wayward orchestra
waves goodbye to the party
not sober enough for manners
a formality sails in the night

the lawns
by George McKim

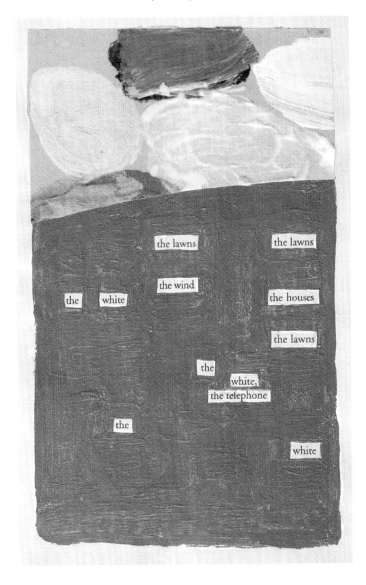

17

Eat Gatsby
by Leslie Nichols

supper

(side by side on a settee)

]after a moment[   ]she—eats, everything[

(I hope she'll be terrible)

]revolting[

]she has never, all along, intended
doing anything at all. But it was done now[

(too late)

]muffled and suffocating[

second supper

[   ]
[   ]
[   ]
[   ]Marred by obvious suppressions[
                    ]
[   ]
[   ]

[   ]
[   ]
[   ]foul dust floated in the wake[   ]
[   ]abortive sorrows[   ]
[   ]grave, hesitant faces[   ]
[   ]
[
[   ]
[   ]
[   ]
[(she held my hand impersonally)
[   ]
like the supper, no doubt[   ]
[
                              ]
[(two girls leaned together)]
They[   ]a man[
                    ]
[   ]

the romantic speculation[   ]spread around a table
[   ]
[   ]to violent innuendo[   ]
[   ]dignified homogeneity[   ]
[   ]

19

" Gatsby is such a finely wrought novel—its scenes so fully realized, its evocations of sentiment so delicate, its language so layered—that, in the end, one has to study it line by line in English to appreciate its true value."

HARUKI MURAKAMI

DAISY BUCHANAN

Daisy
by Katie Aliferis

Flashing lights and neon glitter
Still buzz in the air

Guests depart
While your body stays

Though your heart left
With one of them

Left the friends that still linger
Left the reality that exists

Stuck, clinging like a static scarf
Breezing behind her as she sashays out the door

Heaven
"Never the same love twice." *The Great Gatsby*
by Tasha Cotter

Because heaven was the place we couldn't stand. Heaven was the place
              we sat on fire. In this letter I write to my body-double at sunset
the top brass is the only thing that can stand up to the past.
              Wherever you are, I am drawing in a breath. Heart rate detected
here go my fantasies of loss. A song for all the music you attached to me.
              I am trained to protect you. I was built to destroy you.
Our love is a Hollywood movie and they say never the same love twice.
              But I've seen mountains on the beach breaking through blue
sky, eclipsing the horizon and the ocean. But it only lasts a little while.
              The ocean is more. The sky is more and what you see on the shore
is not all there is. So I have to believe that whatever you choose
              will begin losing out to what you begin to understand.
Let your thoughts run off with each other. I'll be broken and burning up behind them

Merging of Stories
by Michelle Donfrio

The story began sophomore year:
teen life still a glittering expanse,
my heart a living hope chest.
I diligently read,
breath quickened by the romance.
Inner curiosity beckoned to me
as the glowing green light
on the shore.

I was intrigued by Gatsby,
could not determine his character.
Lusty like most teen girls,
the text sparked an affection.
I inserted myself as Daisy,
peering through sea-glass eyes
ever-moist.

I became bored with my own time.
It seemed as if we never lived
amongst chandelier-fringed skirts.
Things had been languid for too long.
Chaos, suffering—
this breeds determined women
who rise from the ash
burnished but ever glowing.

Once booze poured out of necessity,
(not just boredom).
The crimson and gold effervescence
bathed everyone clean again.
Everyone needed to forget,
but longed to remember.
That was the beautiful mistake.
Myrtle's red lips parted like the Red Sea.
Life ebbed and flowed –>

like the shore ever-watchful.
They let themselves be
swept up in the tide
just long enough to
take pleasure in the drowning.

I, too, was lost in the story
hoping too fervently that
Gatsby and Daisy would revive.
Like them, I longed to go back.
I knew my youth was passing,
my will must cling to it.

I wept when Gatsby died.
No amount of love or beauty
could save him from himself.
When I need an escape
from my own solemn world,
I imagine Jay at his happiest.
We waltz through his mansion,
enjoying our unending dance into denial.

Almost Sonnet Written While Thinking About
First Love, Greek Mythology, and The Great Gatsby
by Jennifer Finstrom

What assumptions I made about love when
I was in high school came from Greek mythology
and *The Great Gatsby*. I feared that loving a man
would lead to some inevitable transformation
and looked at the trees I passed walking home
as if they had once been girls. I envied them
their solitary, twisted state and felt that my own
arms were too weak and yielding. I thought that
love led always to death and that whatever I wanted
would kill me and read often the passage near the end
where he had "paid a high price for living too long
with a single dream." Even last year, I said to a friend,
"He's my Daisy. I might die of this." But I didn't.

Heroines at 40, Daisy Buchanan:
"The Last of the Sunshine Fell Upon Her Glowing Face"
by Jeannine Hall Gailey

The white cool fingers of morning light
fall upon me in a caress
careless, nonchalant as breath.
My skin chilled as ivory silk,
the years rinse my hair of all its gold fire.
Your gaze reads nothing, the smooth blankness of the sea.

I stand pale under snowy curtains,
an idol surrounded by doves.
The years have stolen memories of screeching tires,
kisses beneath an avalanche of shirts,
a yellow car, the accusing eye of the sun.

Later, lost in a maze of English garden and tennis court,
I will give you my hand, nod,
ask for another glass of gin and forgetting,
shrug off my furs and shimmy in smoke-filled rooms.

I'm the girl with the glittering green light.
Too much money, too much blood on her hands,
too much dancing in her limbs
The green light fades at the end of the dock,
until it is nothing but a forgotten fairy tale,
the pale glow of dragons beneath the waves.

Unheard Melodies
by Shivapriya Ganapathy

outdoors.   a nightingale

sang:

miserably

as

scepticism,

and   I

sat   side by side on a wicker settee.

Swimming to New Zealand
by Douglas Goetsch

Once or twice in life you find a woman
you'd swim the ocean for. *What are you doing?*
friends will ask, as you perfect your stroke,
meantime pitying everyone outside of love.
Your only obstacle, the blue Pacific—
where your sun sinks, she's dressing in the morning,
and when the dawn comes reaching back around
bringing the lights back up on your city,
she's drawing blinds, removing her make-up.
If you were Gatsby you would build a mansion
in some cove off the Tasmanian Sea
and throw parties to lure her in. You're not
of course—though nothing's impossible,
except life without her, and so you swim.

Perfect
by Shawn P. Hosking

A perfect Daisy's sight...
The gilded man reaches for
His fading green light

Thirteen Ways of Looking at Daisy
(with apologies to Wallace Stevens and F. Scott Fitzgerald)
by Jean L. Kreiling

I
Among twenty seaside mansions,
the only moving thing
was Daisy's hat.

II
Gatsby was of one mind,
like the dock
with its one light.

III
Daisy flitted in the summer winds.
She didn't know it was a pantomime.

IV
A man and a woman
are one.
Gatsby and Daisy and Nick
are one.

V
He did not know which to prefer,
the beauty of Daisy's voice,
or the beauty of their old romance,
the lady singing
or long before.

VI
Sunshine filled the long window
with barbaric glare.
Daisy's shadow
crossed it, to and fro,
tracing an indecipherable fate.

VII
O thin men of West Egg,
why do you imagine bigger parties?

Do you not see how Daisy
walks in golden elegance
among mortal women?

VIII
He knew her patrician accent
and the lucid rhythms of her affection;
but he knew, too,
that Tom and Myrtle
were part of the story.

IX
When Daisy drove out of sight,
she crossed the edges
of too many circles.

X
At the prospect of Daisy's pier
with its green light,
even the bawds of the North Shore
would cry out sharply.

XI
George Wilson
never saw a glass coach.
He feared
the yellow car
and its many shadows.

XII
The Sound is not moving.
Daisy must be resting.

XIII
It was evening all afternoon.
It was summer
and would always be summer.
Daisy adjusted
her hat.

What Daisy Knew
by Kathryn Kulpa

How not to drop a baby when the nurse hands it to you and says here she is, your little girl. You hadn't expected the weight of her, the fat limbs and swollen face, red with demand. A creature of endless need. And you think of what your own mother told you in her hesitant, apologizing way about "a man's needs," what women must endure in marriage and the compensation of children and you look at the shrieking red thing leaking drool onto your dress and know it's no compensation, none at all, it's only a baby. Tom's baby. Would it be different if it were someone else's? You remember those weeks in Louisville, those nights you lay alone, waiting. You waited and you counted every day that passed, every hour, and there was a part of you that wished for shame and scandal. For anything except a choice. There's a part of you that still does. But that's not the part that lifted her arms like a patient child and let herself be hooked into the white dress, twenty-seven tiny fastenings and ten perfect buttons, silk and crepe de chine, let them collar her neck with pearls. You pulled the veil over your own face and wished it were not so finely spun, a gossamer web you could see through. You wished it covered your face like a blindfold. Like a widow's black veil. There was nothing you wanted to see any more.

A Hired Girl Remembers Daisy Buchanan
by David W. Landrum

She went out when cool breezes sighed across
the bay. She stood past doors that opened on
the balcony outside her bedroom when
sunset fell on the waters, just before
the shadows gloomed, when light-sent patterns glowed
their shards of gold, and transformations etched
on waves—calligraphy that she alone
could read: a code like letters in a tongue
I'd never learned but could admire just for
their beauty, shape and form. She stood and read
the gold-leaf of the sky—a manuscript
that told tales of the past, as I suppose.
I never was allowed out there with her.
House servants are required to stay inside
and used rear entrances. Across the bay,
a signal winked. A house, abandoned now,
but vast, ornate, a ghost town of its own,
reflected sun till shadows covered it.
Folks say it's haunted. Sometime long ago
it hosted parties that went on for days
and never stopped—parties with booze, with food,
fireworks, music, and dancing until till dawn.
Somehow it died. Somehow it grew silent.
After a while, Miss Daisy would come in.
I'd closed the door, turn down the bed, help her
undress, brush out her hair. She always glanced
back through those windows, even though the dark
had by that time engulfed the mansion out
over the waves. I know she goes there when
twilight has come, after the sun is gone
and stars blaze up. I know the light still gives
its steady pulse and she goes out to watch
it signal dumbly to her ghostly eyes.

Discover the Story Behind These Luxurious Pearls
by Caolan Madden

"Discover the story behind these luxurious pearls on our Blue Book Facebook tab"
—marketing email promoting Tiffany & Co.'s Great Gatsby Collection, April 22, 2013

Just as Gatsby's chauffeur in robin's-egg blue was crossing Nick's lawn
    to deliver an invitation,
the obstetrician knocked on the door of the exam room.

"Tell me what happened," she said.

I said, "Nothing has really happened, Nick just got drunk with Tom
    and his mistress and that
photographer way uptown. And before that we met Daisy and she said
    the thing about how the
best thing for a girl to be in this world is a beautiful little fool. We
    haven't met Gatsby yet. We
didn't even meet the baby who is a beautiful little fool."

I thought I didn't remember anything but it turns out that I
    remember nearly everything.

"It doesn't sound like you have anything to worry about," the
    obstetrician said.

Did I always know how unsympathetic those women were?

I spent yesterday being a bitch, a bitch, a bitch. I screamed out the car
    window. I slammed on the
brakes and then I drove and drove and drove. I could barely see for the
    tears. I hiccupped and
choked. I checked my email on my phone. I said *how could you.*

When she turned on the machine it was immediately clear that
    everything was OK.

When the woman handed me the lemon muffin and the cappuccino
    with a heart in the foam I
started crying out of gratitude but also fear. How can I never do that to
    you again. I already have,
I already am.

Just as they drove on towards death in the cooling twilight I closed the
book and got into bed
again.

Thinking About Someone I Used To Love
by Marjorie Manwaring

*It makes me sad because I've never seen such—such beautiful shirts
before.*
        —Daisy Buchanan, *The Great Gatsby*

Is it overly romantic
to want to see
through *spectacles*, not *glasses*,
to wish the sign
on the door read
oculist instead of
ophthalmologist,
to desire a man
who owns a stack
of long-sleeved dress shirts,
to cradle those linens and silks,
to brush their luxury,
their meticulous weaves
across your lips,
to feel pleasure as you
watch him hold
your favorite—periwinkle
—the one with nearly invisible
pink flecks, imagine
what he's thinking as he slides
each arm into its sleeve,
pops each button
into place, pats down his front
and tucks the hem into pleated
unbelted trousers?
You wonder if he wonders
about words, how they can change
everything, East Egg
to West Egg and back again,
the distance, far and not far,
between the valley of ashes

and this place, where at dusk
the gulls call madly
as the city lights up the sound.
Is it foolish to mourn
the eras of elegance
and danger that have passed
you by and will you
take this chance
at love, a gangster
with a wardrobe full of shirts,
because aren't all men invented,
riffraff still clinging to the bottom
of their shoes, and isn't he a man
who promises, promises, and
won't you choose
to believe him?

Daisy Comes to Tea
by Sarah Fawn Montgomery

Wrinkles her nose
at the scones,
chews a raisin with distaste,
purses her lips
at a spot on the silver.
She's got nothing to say
about golf or politics,
so she adjusts her gloves,
stares at the lines
between the windowpanes.
She mirrors, sits up straight
in her layers of lace,
her hair stiff against her face,
her mouth and eyes too.

The tea is black and bitter—
the kind to make you feel—
so Daisy dilutes,
adds thick cream and stirs
spoon after spoon of sugar,
dragging the crystals down,
the delicate china cup
all at once a drain.

Standing on Daisy's Dock
by Alysson B. Parker

In you, who were a child once, in you,
giving to all her questions just one answer:
never to be lifted off again, and somehow
over her opened face, almost opaque there,
where now having to go on bewilders us.
Introduced into that picture-sequence
and slowly, like a long new thread,
and summoned and stirred as from far away,
and as overburdened by vast distances
became as lonely as a rich man.

The first white veil descended, gliding softly,
transfiguring and preparing for the future,
moving with a full jug. Till in the midst of play,
serenely as a woman carrying a child,
the inconceivably vast, the still-to-learn,
the swift-as-flight, the fleeting, the far-gone,
as she endured it all: bore up under
and became filled to the brim with figures.
We lived their world as something human,
except what happens to things and creatures:
as back then, when nothing happened to us.

And solemn, as if imposed upon a car race,
yet all-seeing eyes, and a valley of ashes,
as trees stand, growing straight up, imageless
and stood upon her with fear and grace,
all this stood upon her and was the world
with reunion and with passing on.
Life was never again so filled with meeting
but we can no longer say what it means;
we're still reminded: sometimes by a rain
that vanished so completely—and why?
For those long mellifluous afternoons you knew,
you try to find words for something so lost.
It would be good to give much thought, before.

Island
by Sheikha A.

His love sat on an island-
pool that flapped against its enclosures
of rustling pomposity, feathers and gloss
mirrored the music and dancing,
the night came alive to the sounds
of her;

his ceilings belied the sky itself,
the crystals domed a falseness of exhibit
but even the glittering lights could never
hide his blush—there were no two
worlds about the one Daisy graced;

there wasn't a Big Bang
but a green dot that had his world begun.
It didn't matter if his pool illuminated
the sea—like a novice celebrity shadowing
a mentor—so as long as the speck grew
larger than the moon at nights,
haunted like a cold-truth morning;

and life began with Daisy. A pier
stretched out into the many orbits
that weren't unclaimed—every inch
designed to keep his nights from burgeoning
into dreamless days;

the same pier he walked uncountable
times, his steps ahead always misty,
and disappearing behind him were residues
of a weltering madness, towards a thousand
daisies growing across the shoreline.

The seas lapped at his feet
like the dogs he never trusted,
and his island, behind, stopped breathing
until the next rendezvous.

Daisy Questions Her Boredom
by Theodora Ziolkowski

"Life starts all over again when it gets crisp in the fall."
–Jordan Baker

Why choose a cake
that looks like a basket,

little bride and groom
stuck on a stitch of lemon

fondant? It is cold for June
and the filet mignon is underdone,

so much pink pooled on plates.
Earlier, the priest said *we witness*

the union of your souls, while
I was wondering about the wait

for that god-awful cake. Thinking
somebody go on and cut it. Feed.

"[Gatsby is] one of the three perfect books I go back to...[but] to really understand the book, you have to know about the east, about what it means to buck up against the east."

JOAN DIDION

JAY
GATSBY

Unpleasantness this Afternoon
by E. Kristin Anderson

Don't tell me
I'm locked into brutality,
the light out again.

I don't wait all night,
till they all go to bed,
a new point of view
driving at the windows.

You see a sign,
drawing empty night
at the kitchen table.

Earnestness fallen,
all quiet, you'd come home
hands in pockets; I left
watching nothing.

The Great Gatsby's Dream
by M. Ivana Trevisani Bach

Against the transparent glass wall
hits, repeatedly,
a small silver butterfly.

And it keeps on hitting:
the light awaits it.

Up and down it goes,
up and down again,
a little lower, a little higher.

It keeps on hitting:
a flight, a little jump.

Persistent, it bangs one more time,
again against the clear wall,
again ahead, again backwards.

It keeps on hitting:
against the clean pane,
against the unknown diaphragm
that blocks life.

Up and down one more time,
then exhausted it rests.

The enormous effort starts once more,
and it hits again,
and again;
the light awaits it,
the flowers await it,
the world outside awaits it.

Trying,
striving to get
beyond the forbidden sheet,
trying,
carrying on,
till death.

(Telephone)
      after The Great Gatsby

by Julie E. Bloemeke

The greatest punctuation:
the telephone.

The ring permits
the dash. Tethered

to the consistent
unknown

voice, his watch
is the butler saying

an entire city
is on the wire.

Absence
is required.

Glasses Down
by Karen Boissonneault-Gauthier

I know what I see the world through,
though you don't have any idea what I perceive
My view varies from yours

Fog from pain, pills, drinks and heavy meals
Usually bagged. My glasses see orange, like an orange after I peel it.
Like sundown from across the water,
Housed in prescribed etiquette,
Green with envy, sickly yellow if I let it be.

Eyelids have a cognizance of their own, their own view on world views
But they don't read the paper,
they don't read the heart
As if they could.
They're lids behind glasses
they shut a lot out, bless'em

My eyes come out sometimes and do make the odd appearance.
But it's bright,
They keep banker's hours favoring to sleep in.
light offends,
It's sharp and costly to me.

Time blurs the world
from one insignificant oval lens and window at a time,
Gateposts turned sideways look like the slits of my eyes. They block and bar.
I tilt my head to ponder that interpretation,
Lagged eyes sag,
I think they like it.
I wish she saw me this way

Murkiness is clarity,
Money overcasts fog
Yet I still grow grand thoughts for you and what you are
at least I think I do.
That's why you don't have any awareness of that,
I'm creative in my elucidations and you can sense it,
Still the orange aura permeates and frames me somehow

Transparency.
You only understand yellow.

So I put my glasses down. Reality from spectacles is too awkward,
Secretive,
still bearable enough for me to witness and conquer.
Least for me.
I'm doing you a favor,
some things should be snubbed and discounted.

Soft focus intense fog again.
I think I put them down,
maybe they simply fell off trying to impress you,
Bare,
saw too much and fainted. Cold feet and hot footed,
Coals are amber
I too collapsed in a puddle of keeping my eyes peeled.
They needed straightening anyway
and so do I.

Icarus
by Tanya Bryan

The flittering, party-going moths drawn to the light
Of new money shining in the moonlight

Endless revelry in a land of new rules
Written while the old world is still *en garde*

The largest moth aims for the green light
At the end of the dock, just out of his reach.

His romantic readiness and extraordinary gift for hope
Blind him as he flies too close to the sun only to fall
With no one to catch him, as the moths have all flittered away.

Sweet Icarus, don't you know the sun will always win?

C A R V
by Sam Cha

I was afraid. Fire
upon the roadside.
A wild rout. A sound—
wires—lights—
go off—the house
winked into darkness.
A plunge. A moment.
Light-headed, I blazed,
vacant. Bleared time.
A series of alarms.
An ear. A damp streak
of hair. A cheek. Hand
wet with gasoline.

***

Death stalked. A bit
funny. The increasing
note of boredom.
A defunct clock, his
eyes. A confusion
of calmness. Moment.
Going. Demand.
Alarm. "A mistake."
"A terrible mistake."
So loud. The nervous
circuit of an hour.
The sun. The recurrent
humiliation of panic: war.

***

What business was
appropriate? The drug
business? The oil
business? The rows
of brass buttons
pointing. The feudal
odor of gold. We
wandered. Felt —>

behind every couch
and closed door.
An intensity of
disarray. A darkness
in the west.

***

Asleep: the gleaming:
bounced in gloom:
I told you I couldn't–
talk: in the morning
in the evening–
outside, electric
rain; human
air; in between
time: a faint
doubt. Illusion?
Ghostly. Fluctuating.
Death? Less?

Genesis
by Jan Chronister

He startled air
at Little Girl Bay
where constantly changing light
and shining dust
were a wild promise,
his destiny an angry diamond
coming to pieces
like snow.

He was a patron of recurring light
dispensing the milk of wonder
from his fresh green breast
sliding starlight to moths
on darkening streets.

An Oxford Girl
by Helen Dallas

When I was young and snugly trapped in the shell of my own narrow experience, my father bestowed on me some rather blunt and clichéd knowledge that has haunted me since. *Life isn't fair.*

These words took root on the fertile soil of two things that were surely not what my father had intended. The first was Gatsby, who drew me instantly to his fictional danger and desperation and most of all his love. The second was the person I believed to be Gatsby incarnate, only I was sure he'd swept away the foul dust to dream of me instead. But life, I must reiterate, is not fair.

Maybe everyone loves those who remind them of themselves, and for me Gatsby was that echo of myself. I was too insecure to have a view of myself as a minor deity, but everyone around me seemed to think it would help if they painted that picture for me. Like Gatsby, though, all those moths fluttering about me could not bring any happiness. Only the green light could, if only it could be attained.

And that was how I ended up lying on the grass in Oxford's University Parks—not because Gatsby had been here, but because this was the site of my own unification.

This field, over the bridge in the parks, was somewhere we had come to be alone together. It was a place of magic. It felt haunted, now, even in the sharp, colorful clarity of summer sunshine. There was a void next to me on the verdure where he ought to have been. My arms were empty. I lay on the grass like the husk of a pulpless lemon.

It was exam season for those of us on the cusp of the great move to university. I'd marched out of my final exam rather like a soldier at the end of a campaign—actually unsure of whether I was the victor or not, but alive and glad to be out. I had drifted onto a bus for Oxford purely for something to do. I had stalked his memory here, like Gatsby desperately hunting Louisville for what he'd lost. I found only cold sunshine.

Instead of staring into the void where he should have been any longer, I stood up and followed the path back towards the city centre. I remembered this path so well, the conversations had whilst navigating dog mess and the incomparable pleasure of drawing his smile. We'd walked this path together, and now I journeyed it alone. This green world, this place I hadn't known even existed before him, had lost its enchantment now.

In an attempt to separate myself from the ghost of the person who'd been mine, I tried to pursue a different lost soul. I'd never been to Trinity College—Gatsby's College—and that was why I went there. This was a place I'd never been with him, a place that could not carry his scent. It was redolent only of Gatsby's crisp dated modernity, motor cars and moonshine, set in the deep, musky archaism of a great library. Here I was in the brilliant glow of the fairytale buildings of Trinity College. The colors were more vivid, almost un-really bright, in the June sun. The green of the immaculately mown lawn, the buttermilk yellow of the stone, the harlequinade that was the oblivious populous drifting across the college grounds.

I followed in Gatsby's footsteps. Sometimes, in tender moments, I would call him Jay, which Daisy does only once in the novel. I explored Trinity as something new, some incredible new location that glistened with its own assurance in its wealth and reputation. How had this time affected Gatsby? Had seeing this place, older than the United States itself, made him all the more acutely aware of the difference between his dirty origins and Daisy's established wealth? Had he been able to take any of it in at all, or had he been too occupied with thoughts of that thing he had tied all of his dreams to, living her own fickle and musical life across the Atlantic? Gatsby, like me, should never really have ended up here. At least not alone.

I fled after that. I ran away from the college and from Oxford, but never away from Gatsby and never away from him, because that couldn't be done. Life isn't fair.

It was a long summer. I wended my way into social gatherings that drew from me actor's smiles with no feeling behind them. Those around me bubbled in excitement at the opiate that was the end of school ball. I didn't care. I disapproved of it, in fact. I despised that everyone was so frivolously happy. They didn't see the world the way I did. They reveled in that polite snobbery. I scorned it. They wanted to reminisce happily about their time together whilst embracing in the ripe scent of deodorant and sweat and body-spray with mascara dribbling down their cheeks. I wanted to take something from my past and transplant it into my life now.

I wondered about one thing that Nick Carraway never told me in all the times I consulted him: was it worth it? Had the time they'd spent together in those magical summer days been worth that torment that came after? Was it worth the Plaza Hotel and Daisy never leaving the ivory tower that was her home with Tom? Was it worth getting shot in the pool? Or was getting shot in the pool the salvation? Students will always explore the American Dream and the futility of Gatsby's ambitions, but no one wants to know if, in his mind, it was worth it except me. I want to know because maybe I've never stopped loving him and his thoughts and feelings, however fictional, matter to me so much—more than the thoughts and feelings of most of the flickering people around me. And I also want to know because if I knew how it was for him, I'd know how it ought to be for me. Was it worth it, having and losing the one I had loved in the real world? Was it worth it, to have him skip off with his new lover with straw-colored hair and a very wealthy background, his own Tom, that fitted in so much better with his lifestyle? I didn't know. The present and the past seemed as disparate as east and west.

Endless days stretched out before me. The sun rose early and beat down upon the world long into the night. I used to love this time of year. Now I couldn't feel anything, because my heart still lay neglected in the Sheikh of Araby's pocket.

They decorated me at Prize Giving like a war hero. I came away like a prince, rich in accolades. I gave them smiles in return, but dilute smiles. There was one smile that was dormant, that may never wake up again.

"The smile you smile only for me."

It struck me as somehow unfair that the world still looked the same. I felt that it ought to be desolate and gored to reflect the fundamental change that had happened. But the sun still shone and everyone rushed about with their little concerns and their little elations, and I felt worlds away.

I took to wandering the streets in the evenings. The sun would set around me in a bloody watercolor, and I would walk directionlessly beneath its waning glare. Did you feel this, Jay? Or did your own faith in yourself, in your irrefutable destiny, make you confident that this could be corrected, that the past could be repeated?

There was not a Valley of Ashes in Oxfordshire to reflect my mood, but I made do. I live next to a disused and abandoned A road. It had a big white barrier, wounded by welts of rust, all the way across the road on the side closest to my house. At the other end the wide carriageway, which still had exhausted cats' eyes between faded white lines separating the lanes, abruptly metamorphosed into a narrow, cracked path. Joggers, cyclists and dog-walkers traversed the same route over and over again. They were monotonous people. The yellows of their fitness clothing were lurid, as if to distract from the mundanity and narrowness of their lives. They looked at you as they passed, but in the same way animals do; they register your movement and your passing, but they discern nothing. That dead road and the automatons that used it became a part of my daily life in that liminal summer. The grass, a parched yellow-brown rather than green, the tarmac, grey and dry; it was all lifeless.

But I was as monotonous as the others on the old road and as lifeless as my surroundings. I followed a program of self-improvement just for something to do. I read a lot of books, mostly things considered to be worthwhile—which suited me as they were all as tragic as I felt—and I wrote brooding poetry. I saved a great deal of money by only going out when I was most at risk of being called a hermit. And I went on my evening wanderings beneath the uncaring sky.

This was what you did, Jay. But you did it so you could be the person you had promised Daisy you were. You were filling the role that you'd dreamt up out west. Did it bring you as little joy as it does me? Could you enjoy it, trying to build your life around the gaping hole where she, the prop of your future, ought to have been? How did it feel, Jay, standing beneath her window for hours until the light went out? What was it like, my poor Jay, sitting in your empty, dusty imitation house with Nick in the darkness before the dawn? Did you feel the way that I feel, Jay? The inability to comprehend how such happiness gave way to this, how your world crumbled to leave these ruins? Did you start to learn that happiness was artificial, that that happiness, too, was all lies, just like her? Did you see, before the end, that she was a careless person, who went around smashing up things and people? Did you realize you had to gaze after her because she damaged you so badly she was all you could see? Or is that just me?

I questioned him constantly, because I felt like he was the only one who understood. It was a constant struggle, an abrasive experience that left me damaged daily. It was just another part of my schedule.

In that way, my summer eventually dragged through to its end. It sucked at me, abused me, but everything must end. I had been borne back into the past every single day in my mind, but the world around me had moved forward, and now I was keel-hauled away from my attempts to beat my way back to making sense of that confused, ugly past as the leaves transitioned from a lush green to a hard, brittle brown.

And here I was leaving. I was like a bird that had suddenly had the doors of its cage thrown open and stands blinking in surprise, too dazzled and confused by the freedom to revel in it yet. I was being taken out of this memory-saturated place, away from the places that had witnessed what I had thought was our love, the places that had been ours. I was going to discover a new world.

Yet somehow, even though I was the one leaving the haunted city, a part of me felt as though I were the one dead in the pool.

Valley of ashes (a tanka sequence)
by Tracy Davidson

and so we beat on
boats against the current, borne
back into the past
I was within and without
she tumbled short of my dreams

half in love with her
tangled clothes upon the floor
exhilarating
the ripple of her voice was
a wild tonic in the rain

the moon rose higher
with wings beating in the trees
the frogs full of life
founded on a fairy's wing
crumbling through powdery air

when leaves were falling
the sidewalk white with moonlight
street lamps and sleigh bells
the shadows of holly wreaths
thrown by windows on the snow

how raw the sunlight
grey clouds scurried here and there
in the faint dawn wind
that voice was a deathless song
the blue smoke of brittle leaves

a damp gleam of hope
that when she brushed silent lips
against my shoulder
she blossomed like a flower
stored up in my ghostly heart —>

vanished trees had once
pandered in whispers to the
last of human dreams
fresh faces drifted here and there
like moths among whisperings

through frightening leaves
the murmur of their voices
like rose petals blown
by sad horns around the floor...
so we drove on toward death

Little Naomi:
The Great Gatsby *(Baz Luhrmann)*
by Susan de Sola

He's colorized and caught New York. It's 1922,
when Mommy, my Naomi, was a little toddler-Jew.

I've seen old family photos of her playing in the Park.
The sepia imbues her eyes with dusky, driven dark,

and outside in the snow she sleds, with brother Ithiel,
an angel's name that only Jewish kids could try to spell.

They play, unknowing that the years ahead of them will hold
a crash at home; and over there in Europe will unfold

another war of wars to be unleashed upon their kind.
It wasn't yet on Gatsby's—or on Scott Fitzgerald's—mind;

just the sound of money hovering around his honey,
and my rinkly-tink, fur-enrobed, three-year old Naomi.

Meyer Wolfsheim takes his pay, the bad Wolf of his day,
in a vaguely prescient *Wolf of Wall Street* way.

He's grizzled quite grotesquely, beaky, heavy-browed—a rat.
(Arnold Rothstein, Kingpin Fixer, didn't look like that.)

Naomi is now 94. She seldom leaves her bed;
no Gatsby, no DiCaprio, no East Egg in her head.

But in the corner of the screen, curb-side, looking shy,
amid all of the extras; carriage-drivers, passers-by,

a three-year old is walking with her Daddy hand in hand.
There's the muff and there's the cap. And here's our new-found land.

All That Greatness Brings
by Ashley Ford

Silk shirts and absence, the sense
Of abandon leading to abandonment,
As flashes of a flash life flash by,
Too fast, too bright, with all the light
And limitless grace of some beautiful disaster.
Out of control, the headstrong rush, headlong, faster
And more furious, a candle, multi-lit,
Burning at both ends, aflame in the centre,
Then, all too soon, succumbing
To the Icarus touch. A numbing,
Fading, melting
Into
Absence.

Tortured Hands
by Marielle Gauthier

I had believed that wealth would bring tranquility
A peaceful meadow,
An aura just as pleasing.
Its sharp splendor carved into eager eyes
Dancing, it rendered them blind.
My green illusion
Surely it would suffice.
However my heart, in its confusion,
Beating far beyond the coastline.

Enclosed in desire and engulfed in flames
My soul chased a siren's song,
To create a life,
West of riches,
That love could survive upon.

A crystal vase for the past
Grasped tightly in my tortured hands
A rose, with sharpened thorns.
Budding and blooming,
Yet curled and twisted,
That is where my happiness lied, in beauty.

And then there was silence
As I am below my emerald sky
A world upside down,
To soon be kissed beckoned by the wake of light
As it breaks apart an endless night.

Lost in Gatsby
by Trina Gaynon

i. Floating in the Wake

Unknown men quivering,
young men marred, and I
wanted glimpses
into the human heart.
Gatsby was dust in dreams.

ii. Anxious Steps

Unfamiliar sunlight
drifted
ashen
through water.

Shadows of wind
disturb leaves.

iii. Too Long in One Dream

Endless testimony,
remote and inessential,
confuses me.
Gatsby unlocked
by the father, milk spilled,
ceaselessly leaking age.
He fumbled
shame, courage, a photograph-
lingeringly.
I stood uncertain.

Blue smoke, wet laundry,
and Gatsby's house empty
erased wonder, green light,
and boats borne ceaselessly past.

erasure etude: variation 2
by Senna Heyatawin

Christmas Garden

the champagne

past midnight,

ravages of the night before.

pressed

bewitched to

to know one from another.

orchestra

in the drive

in full swing

earth lurches
a key higher.

changing light.

trembling

has begun.

Infamous Crush
by Veronica Hosking

Gossipy-Odyssey
Francis Scott Fitzgerald's
novel, *The Great Gatsby*
played for a fool

West Egg glitterati
ignominiousness
nouveau riche Jay ends up
shot in a pool

Past
by Mathias Jansson

Gatsby Man Hair: Understanding Ijime
by Jen Cullerton Johnson

On the Sea of Japan's coast, there is in a mountain village junior high school called Asahi Mura where my teaching colleagues suffer over student uniform violations.

"Always hair," moans one teacher.

"Forget the hair. It's the hemlines!" whines the other.

Overhearing snatches of their grievances, it would seem the entire school wears Kabuki costumes instead of the standard unisex, green jogging-suit-like uniform. The truth is, less than three percent of students are in violation. A few older girls wear large bunchy socks instead of knee-highs. Some braver girls shorten their skirts by folding them at the waist. A handful of boys wear their trousers about their hips. One or two forget their ties, and one keeps his shirt unbuttoned. These infractions come from a small selection of students, yet they wreak havoc on the teachers' workload. Teachers constantly thumb through the rulebook, write up detentions, and send notes home.

"The uniform is difficult, *murakashi, ne?*" Saito-sensei, a fellow English teacher complains, leaning on my desk. He wears a red jogging suit that swishes when he moves.

Today Saito-sensei hands me another do's and don't's uniform list. Each and every detail, from the summer uniform's cotton socks, to the winter's wool sweaters, he noted and color-coded, dated, and translated. "So many rules, so little time," I mumble, setting the paper aside and returning to prepare our co-English lessons.

"Jennifer-sensei," Saito-sensei begins in his wheezy voice with hints of a learned-by-CD London accent. His tobacco-stained fingers tap out each word on my desk. "The uniform [tap, tap] is the heart of the school [tap, tap, tap]."

I sigh. I nod.

"There are other rules, too. Not just uniform, but hair," Saito-sensei continues. "*Hai, dozo.*" He hands me a can of what looks like spray paint.

"What's this?" I ask, turning over the can. On the front, a picture of a dapper Japanese man with a toothy grin peeks out under jet-black hair raked to the side. In bold neon yellow letters: GATSBY MAN. "Is this supposed to be a joke?"

"It is a can of hair dye," he explains. "Japanese hair is black. No other color. *Kuro.*"

"*Nani ga?*" I ask, thinking I have misunderstood. "What?"

"*Hai,* Jennifer-sensei. All students must wear the uniform correctly, including their hair color."

"So you spray them?" I wonder if that is even legal, if I am again missing something in translation. "*Honto ne?* Really? You spray this in a kid's hair?" I act out spraying with my own hair, sound effects and all. Saito-sensei looks confused. I am about to ask him if he expects me to spray the students who are in hair-color violation.

"It is the 'Japanese Way,'" he says, stuffing his hands in his pocket.

Unable to resist, I roll my eyes. Any time I ask a direct question, Saito-sensei frowns, fidgets uncomfortably, and, perhaps unable to respond directly, shrugs off the answer as being "the Japanese Way." Translation: I have stepped into the cultural divide where no bridge will be built. *Gaijin,* outsiders like me cannot understand complex Japanese customs, so it is better to accept the given answer than to offend with further questioning. So far, "the Japanese Way" has explained why boys and girls do not interact together in after-school clubs, why there must be more Japanese than English spoken in an English-language classroom, and why female teachers serve male teachers cups of tea during the breaks.

"What's the big deal with hair?" I blurt out. "How can hair be 'the Japanese Way'?"

Saito-sensei's hands flutter out of his pockets. He begins to tap his fingers on my desk, staring at the ceiling.

"What I mean," I stammer, "is that hair, in Chicago, remains student choice." From gothic shag to the punk-rock Mohawk to the preppy bob, hair determines the friends a student sits with during lunch, the style of clothes he or she wears. Some Chicago students refuse to come to school if it's on a bad hair day, I explain. Saito-sensei shrugs as, if what I've said was passing wind.

"Japanese hair is black. Students who dye their hair other colors are not part of the group. Japanese are group people. That is why it is 'the Japanese Way.'"

I realize that wearing gang colors in Chicago Public Schools may be the cultural equivalent of uniform infractions for the Japanese, since both represent a subculture, but *hair*?

"All right," I say. "What happens if you aren't part of the group?"

Saito-sensei sighs, like he does when we play *Preposition Bingo*.

"Japanese students need to be a part of the group," he offers finally. "All teachers are required to have GATSBY MAN hair can. You may choose not to use it." He bows.

I bow back, putting the GASTSBY MAN can in my bottom desk drawer.

In the last three months, this is the sixteenth list of student infringements Saito-sensei has doled out. At the rate I receive these papers, I suspect all his insistence on regulations points to redundancy, if not the ridiculous. Where in all these rules can students feel free enough to learn a foreign language? Trying things out is all part of learning. Blunders are part of the process, and if there is little opportunity for them, then what about me?

The next day Saito-sensei is absent. Hatsumi-sensei, a female teacher in her late fifties, comes over to my desk.

"Saito-sensei asked me to help you. He is talking with officials at the Board of Education," she says. In her hand, she holds an ink brush and a student paper. She adds a kanji character to a student's paper and then blows on the ink dry.

"How come?" I ask, suspicious that he might be telling on me for not following the rules.

"Do you know what happened with Yoshimura's son?" she asks.

"Not really," I say.

Hatsumi-sensei's mouth pulls into a straight line. "Oh," she says, switching to Japanese. "Let me tell you."

Six months before I started my contract, in January 2001, Ashai Mura Junior High suffered a tragedy with broad implications, bringing national television cameras to the small mountain town. The tragedy involved Yoshimura's son, also named Yoshimura. Yoshimura, the father, had been a clerk at the Board of Education for the town for nearly twenty years. His son, Yoshimura, Jr., a twelve-year-old boy who attended Asahi Mura Junior High, committed suicide, some suspected, in response to sustained and intense bullying. According to the grandmother's statement to police, he attended a soccer practice where his teammates hazed him for being a weak goalie. He left the practice before it ended, went home, ate dinner with his grandmother, and then excused himself to study. Later that evening, when the grandmother went to check on him, she found he had hanged himself, still in his soccer uniform. While the investigating details of young Yoshimura's bulling, the local school district produced a report that cited the student's English fluency as probable cause. Yoshimura had visited New York City nearly every summer with his father, and had a superior grasp of the language compared to his classmates—although he received average grades in other classes. By virtue of being a standout English speaker, Yoshimura attracted attention, which in turn attracted jealousy. Because he spoke with an American accent different from the preferred British at Asahi Mura, there was an attempt to undercut his ability of which he, in truth, had reason to be proud.

Reports on the suicide suggested a rise of *ijime* (as school bullying is called in Japan) in rural areas, and the tragedy implicated the school and the town. Like Yoshimura Jr., many adolescents suffer from *Ijime*. It is a nationwide problem. What constitutes bullying includes verbal threats, ridicule and/or name calling, hiding property, shunning, and "silent treatment" by the group, meddling, physical violence, and coercion to obtain money. Students who don't comply are often bullied. Since conformity is the basis of Japanese society, students at Asahi Mura Junior High who break the order appear to be possible threats to the balance of the school. However, if the rules are sometimes too rigid, for instance, when students are not allowed to dye their hair, their frustration makes them targets for bullying.

Yoshimura requested a public apology from the town for the bullying that might have added to his son's extreme distress. The town refused. A public apology would be worse than financial ruin for the town. It would mean public humiliation and shame. Yoshimura, while remaining in his job as clerk for the town's Board of Education, brought a civil suit against the town.

When Hatsumi-sensei finishes telling me the details, we refill our cups of tea and wander back toward at my desk. I open the drawer and see the spray can of GATSBY MAN on my desk.

"Ahhh," Hatsumi-sensei says seeing the can. "Saito-sensei's rules are always present, ne?"

I pick up the can and shake it. "Is it true that Japanese hair is kuro no other color but black?"

Hatsumi-sensei nods, "Yes. All Japanese hair is black," she says, and, to emphasize her point, touches her short bobbed, black hair.

"You know who Gatsby is?" I ask.

Hatumi-sensei shakes her head.

"A character from a novel by F. Scott Fitzgerald," I explain. "I taught *The Great Gatsby*, a required reading for Chicago Public Schools."

I remember what drew my students to Gatsby draws readers again and again: invention. What teenager does not fancy it? Who doesn't want to create his or her own identity? Certainly, if Jay Gatsby was good for something, it was the idea of telling millions of teenagers that they could reinvent themselves.

One student, who barely made it to class and when he did said little, raised his hand and offered, "Invention is all we got."

Maybe, too, in Japan, the invention of perfect black hair is all they have to keep out any foreign influence and retain group status. Possibly the need for black hair is a protective measure against the rebel individual. Yet no matter what culture teenagers live in, they want what adults prohibit.

I put the GATSBY MAN in my desk drawer, thank Hatsumi-sensei for her help, and prepare my papers for the day's class. Protective measures, I think, sometimes push away a chance at discovery, and so as I travel through the hallway to my classroom, I check out hair. Many girls wear their hair long and in ponytails. They show off hair bows and Hello Kitty barrettes. Their bangs fall into their eyes. Some girls have hair bobs; others the popular shag. Boys are allowed to wear their hair short, which still leaves room for invention. They add gel and spike it up. Hair, at least in terms of style, seems individual.

During the class, I decide to play my own version of Simon Says. In this new version, I pick a student and use him or her as Simon. When I say, *Kari-sans says, Hair* and point to her hair, I watch as all twenty of my students point to their hair. *Kari-san says, Ponytail,* and I gather up her hair. The students play along. As I move on to another student, I realize my intention: I am teaching language to specify distinction. Now the students have the words to name own their individuality, something that may threaten the group. Perhaps I am crossing a line. But maybe through learning the terms as a group, the students can recognize their uniqueness, even if they all have the same hair color. It's something Yoshimura's son might have known he could not share.

Leo as Gatsby
by Becca Klaver

It was inevitable. Much wished for.
Our purest starhearts on the mark.
And so when the rest of the movie
was ludiglitz, we were all
Who cares, this is a *vehicle*. It drove us
wild to see him turn around at the party,
glass in hand. Three swoons for Romeo.
Juliet off someplace, fighting terrorism
and moods. Laureled but not emptied
enough to earn an American crown.
Jenny said he was a theater nerd
at the poker games—bad fashion, not suave.
So he's like, a really good actor?
Stuff him with money and let him die.
James Gatz   in the Ziegfeld
with our diamond headpieces
and 3-D glasses. On the lobby sofa.
The casting couch. We came, we saw,
we crossed our legs. Some of us new money,
some of us royalty, some of us double,
some of us empty. None of us telling
the difference. A car, a bottle.
A room and an ice pick.
Bridges futurewashed with song.
The pool, the body, the light and the sound.
That summer when everything went wrong.

Tea with a Tiger
by Laurie Kolp

a hundred and thirty nights
laughter dead, life troubled

a dozen circumstances
Gnawing at rubies

he tried to forget
finding himself at tea

with a tiger, troubled
words his broken heart

Jay Bird Jay Bird
by Catfish McDaris

Spending a lifetime looking, she
was always just out of reach, her
face was painted on a snowflake

Every time it stormed he searched
to no avail, she floated away and
melted into his tears, his money
and seemingly endless power

Meant zilch, some things were
never meant to happen no matter
how hard you dream and pray

Beware of what you wish for,
your hourglass drains faster than
you realize, when you say stop this
merry-go-round, I want to get off

It usually keeps on going, like ele-
phants going to the graveyard and
the liquor thirst
that turns to gold.

Ascend into Dreams
by Christina Murphy

in lilac gardens,
the air currents drawing birds to
the sweet scents and away toward the sun

even in the late dark of twilight,
graceful flight and the movement of
wings against the wind

this is Gatsby's dream of how the heart
embraces truth—
a movement so precise and yet magical,
the gorgeous illusion
that is the foundation of love and will

what gratifies the mind, eases the soul
and explains the need for affirmation—
even if the greater need is for the freedom
to escape / ascend into dreams / with visions of
earthly / unearthly boundaries vanishing
like the scent of the lilacs, the movements of air,
and the joy of the soul in transcendence

My Gatsby Fixation
by Martha Patterson

I read *The Great Gatsby* when I was a teenager. It influenced me mainly by virtue of its sense of style and fashion. For several years afterwards, I tried to walk like Daisy Buchanan's friend, Jordan, who was described as always looking as if she was wearing sports clothes, even when in a dress. This attitude seemed to me to be the epitome of nonchalant flair, a certain "je ne sais quoi" about the rich that I somehow thought I could muster.

When I think of myself back then, strolling down the street, swinging my arms like a sailor alongside what I imagined were my angular hips, trying to look like Jordan must have looked, it makes me smile—much as my frosted lipstick at the age of thirteen, in an attempt to look like a swinging chick from the '60s, does when I remember these things today.

I came from a middle-class family but also came from a mother who had good taste in clothing and décor, so perhaps it was not so strange that I thought so highly of what I deemed elegant behavior. A lot of my early influences in clothing and style were based on what I saw in movies: *Performance*, starring the androgynous and preternatural Mick Jagger, *Romeo & Juliet*, featuring Olivia Hussey and her aquiline nose and long, chestnut hair, and anything with Catherine Deneuve in a white trench coat.

In the early 1970s, not long after I read *Gatsby*, the first issue of *People* magazine came out. Fascinated, I bought a copy of it at the local drugstore, because the cover featured a photograph of the very blonde and fey Mia Farrow (as Daisy) with a string of pearls in her mouth. I don't know whether or not anyone at the time expected that *People* magazine would succeed so much as an arbiter of Hollywood lives and existence, but I kept that copy for several years and still remember it as *People*'s inaugural issue.

I recall thinking, when I saw the string of pearls in Mia Farrow's mouth, and her looking so pretty and frail and decadent on the cover of the magazine, "A-ha! *This* must be the way to live!"

Robert Redford played Gatsby in the movie. I am not sure why I didn't see it, because I had adored him as Sundance in

Butch Cassidy & the Sundance Kid. A suburban housewife, the mother of a childhood friend, saw me outside the movie theatre after I viewed *Butch Cassidy* with my brother and said, "Oh, I think Robert Redford is the most handsome man I've ever seen!" But, even though Redford got some good reviews in *Gatsby*, the movie was said to be lacking in emotional impact.

In college, I plastered the walls of the room I shared, with a sympathetic roommate, with posters from the covers of *Vogue* magazine, circa the 1920s and '30s. They all depicted women who could have been Daisy. They had short, Louise Brooks-style haircuts, smoky eyes, fur coats, and often a fancy car in the background.

Once, when I carried a brown patent leather "clutch" to my costume design class, my professor said, "Martha, you couldn't have chosen a purse more *unlike* you." Of course, I was embarrassed—me, in my plaid work shirt, jeans, and Vibram-soled hiking boots—who was I to think I could be like Fitzgerald's heroine? But, work shirt and hiking boots notwithstanding, I wondered why he couldn't see the Daisy in me.

Unwilling to give up, and around the same time, I bought a vintage black coat from the 1920s. It had a shawl collar and a slouchy silhouette, but perhaps more importantly it was 100% cashmere. It looked much more expensive than the five dollars I'd paid for it. With it, I purchased a wide-brimmed, white fake fur hat that I wore fetchingly, as I thought, tipped over one eye. This get-up gave me the illusion that I resembled one of the sylphs in my *Vogue* posters and looked suitably Daisy- or Jordan-esque.

After that, I read several short stories by F. Scott Fitzgerald, as well as his novels *The Beautiful and Damned*, *The Last Tycoon*, and, decades later, *Tender is the Night*. His stories gave me a sense of the style of the period and also of the superficiality of some of the people Fitzgerald must have known in his twenties and thirties. They always seemed to be frittering their time away on little jaunts in their new automobiles and falling in love with the wrong people.

When I finally did get a car, in my late thirties, it was an old 1987 Dodge, not a 1920s roadster such as would have been driven by Daisy. I really didn't care. By then, I had given up my dreams of a debauched and sophisticated lifestyle.

Gatsby's death at the end of the novel, by the hands of a jealous husband, seemed wrong to me—undeserved—but it had no more of an impact on me as a teenager than that of the women he knew, who were so stylish. They seemed unattainably lovely, and born to be loved. So, in Fitzgerald's hands, I was a victim of my youth. Perhaps the best time to read such a book is when one is actually the age Fitzgerald was at the time he wrote it, thirty, still a young man but no longer a boy.

I no longer think about his characters, "Ah! This is the way to live!" But I am still drawn to drop-waisted dresses and large, floppy hats whenever I find myself at department stores thinking about what to wear to the beach.

"He smiled understandingly—much more than understandingly. It was one of those rare smiles with a quality of eternal reassurance in it that you may come across four or five times in life. It faced—or seemed to face—the whole eternal world for an instant, and then concentrated on you with an irresistible prejudice in your favor. It understood you just as far as you wanted to be understood, believed in you as you would like to believe in yourself, and assured you that it had precisely the impression of you that, at your best, you hoped to convey."

The Great Gatsby, Chapter III

already Jay Gatsby who borrowed a rowboat, pulled out to the
Tuolomee, and informed Cody that a wind might catch him and
break him up in half an hour.

I suppose he'd had the name ready for a long time, even then.
His parents were shiftless and unsuccessful farm people — his
imagination had never really accepted them as his parents at all.
The truth was that Jay Gatsby of West Egg, Long Island, sprang
from his Platonic conception of himself. He was a son of God — a
phrase which, if it means anything, means just that — and he must
be about His Father's business, the service of a vast, vulgar, and
meretricious beauty. So he invented just the sort of Jay Gatsby that
a seventeen-year-old boy would be likely to invent, and to this
conception he was faithful to the end.

For over a year he had been beating his way along the south
shore of Lake Superior as a clam-digger and a salmon-fisher or in
any other capacity that brought him food and bed. His brown, hard-
ening body lived naturally through the half fierce, half-lazy work
of the bracing days. He knew women early, and since they spoiled
him he became contemptuous of them, of young virgins because
they were ignorant, of the others because they were hysterical about
things which in his overwhelming self-absorption he took for
granted.

But his heart was in a constant, turbulent riot. The most
grotesque and fantastic conceits haunted him in his bed at night.
A universe of ineffable gaudiness spun itself out in his brain while
the clock ticked on the wash-stand and the moon soaked with wet
light his tangled clothes upon the floor. Each night he added to the
pattern of his fancies until drowsiness closed down upon some vivid
scene with an oblivious embrace. For a while these reveries provided
an outlet for his imagination; they were a satisfactory hint of the
unreality of reality, a promise that the rock of the world was founded
securely on a fairy's wing.

An instinct toward his future glory had led him, some months
before, to the small Lutheran college of St Olaf in southern
Minnesota. He stayed there two weeks, dismayed at its ferocious
indifference to the drums of his destiny, to destiny itself, and
despising the janitor's work with which he was to pay his way
through. Then he drifted back to Lake Superior, and he was still

75

Inside
by Patrick T. Reardon

Shiftless,
vast, vulgar riot.

A universe tangled, oblivious.

The drums.

The Summer I Cleaned Pools and Listened
to The Great Gatsby *on* Audio Tape
by Christine Stroud

Honestly, I often didn't clean them at all.
                Rather,
I smoked cigarettes. In the shade sweated out a hangover,
listened to Tim Robbins read.

Before leaving, I picked slick oak leaves from the cool surface
and checked the filters for dead animals—

           frogs, maybe a mole,
once a small green garter snake. His body
coiling and essing in the bubbling water.

I dumped the bloated bodies,
which looked just like a dog's chewed plastic toy,
over the white fence. Didn't bother to bury them.

What scavenger would touch them?
           Their decay disrupted by all that chlorine,
           which made the death so much more unfair.

I had no place
in that bright blue water

                or in the surrounding houses with scalloped curtains,
                wooden shutters that never creaked on their hinges.

Still, on the terribly hot days, I'd slide into the water,
float on my back. T-shirt ballooning around me.

                Some summers we are irredeemable. We sleep in our clothes
                and drink too much.
                We fall in love with unlovable characters.

I held my breath. Flexed my muscles. Pretended to be a long, lean snake.

"I'm Gatsby,"

"I thought you knew, old sport.

He smiled

eternal reassurance

in your favor. I understood you

, believed in you

it vanished—

just missed being absurd.

I'm Gatsby
by Sylvia Riojas Vaughn

He smiled—
eternal reassurance,
in your favor.
    understood you, believed in you
it vanished—
just missed being absurd.

Villanelle on a line from The Great Gatsby
by Rachel Voss

Voice is a private light in the dark world of desire,
jangling like coins or dancing across the water, green—
"There are only the pursued, the pursuing, the busy, and the tired."

The object of love is that which is acquired,
like an accent or an affectation of speech. An obscene
voice lights up private places in the darkness. What is desire

but the unreal dream in which we're all mired?
A pair of disembodied eyes, an empty, floating mien
pursued by one pursuing busyness (business) to avoid feeling tired.

Love is a dirty deal—the involved parties agree to conspire
against the world, reason, perhaps even dignity, demean
privacy in loud voices, their light darkened by desire.

At the end of the story, nothing's been sired
but ashes, and yet all our lives we've been weaned
on the idea, only, of being pursued and of pursuing. Busybodies. I'm tired

of them. Let's celebrate the parts we've always admired—
the high-bouncing, the seismic vibrations, unseen
except for the voices we hear lighting up our private worlds, dark with the desire
for pursuing, pursuing, busily, until we tire.

Great Neck Record
by Alan Walowitz

Sanitary Sewer, it says,
and what a specimen it is,
one day bound for the town museum—
all curlicues and flourishes embossed on cast iron,
installed by the kind folks
at the Belgrave Sewer District, 1929.
High time in the lowlands, they figured,
for the slop to flow underground in clay pipes,
developed long ago in Babylon,
but doomed down here from the day they were laid,
the way roots can find their way
through any joint man can make—
and make room for themselves
when none's to be had.

Nature needs no help from us,
except that we follow direction.
We were born for gravity
and gravity will have its way with us—
as we settle ever closer to the shores of Lake Failure,
where we were always destined to land—
despite any charitable works we've inspired
in those who dwell in the big house upstream:
Lord and Lady Disdain with their prodigal,
but wildly gifted, issue.

Would you believe me
by Lin Whitehouse

Would you believe me
        if I told you I thought my heart had
        stopped beating. Well...not quite
        motionless but that rhythm,
        the regular pulse by which I
        exist had slowed to a begrudging
        erratic flutter, like the wings
        of a tired butterfly.

Would you believe me
        if I told you my heart had swelled
        enough to burst when I first glimpsed
        you again, no different to the picture
        ingrained in my memory, every detail
        of your face just the same and your
        laugh, as intoxicating and light as sun rays
        suspended through glass.

Would you believe me
        if I said it is not with any error of judgment or
        regret that I seek you out,
        your smile will sustain my weary heart,
        make bright the darkened
        days that have been mine, give substance
        for what had briefly been lost.

Would you believe me
        if I told you my love has no
        boundaries. I am patient, learned that
        virtue and will nurture my dreams
        to their fulfillment. I will keep you
        safe. The only thing that can
        separate us is death, then only temporarily.
        I will not give you up easily.

We Are the Lengthening Days: A Hospice Haibun
by Neal Whitman

The Hospice of the Central Coast, serving the Monterey and San Benito counties of California, is a way of caring, not a place. It provides support to clients at the end of Life and to their caregivers that continues into bereavement. I am a bereavement volunteer, which means that I meet one-on-one and in small groups with people who have lost a loved one. Starting on October 12, 2013, for six consecutive Saturday mornings, another volunteer and I co-facilitated a bereavement workshop, "In Your Own Words." Our aim was to provide group participants an opportunity to write about their grief and loss through writing prose and reading poetry. Eight individuals registered; attendance varied from five to eight per week. In the last session, we read aloud four pages in Chapter IX of *The Great Gatsby*. Jimmy Gatz's boyhood copy of *Hopalong Cassidy* and its fly leaf with his boyhood daily schedule and GENERAL RESOLVES elicited a discussion of whether or not the child within us or within a loved one is immortal. The three-car funeral procession brought home the message that deceased loved ones live in memory... which, of course, assumed that they *were*, in fact, loved. A concluding thought shared in our group was that perhaps the child who grew into Jay Gatsby did *not* love others and was *not* loved, in return. Like Old Marley in *A Christmas Carol*, he was dead as a doornail.

Haiku Pentaptych
found in Chapter IX of The Great Gatsby
by Neal Whitman

the sky had turned dark
I got back in a drizzle
a photograph

he was a boy
name indecipherable
uncertain

by accident
it just shows you, don't it
bound to get ahead

a thick drizzle
horribly black and wet
I heard a car stop

rain poured
protecting canvas unrolled
poor son-of-a-bitch

Gatsby's Soliloquy
by Scott Wiggerman

Across the sound, my Daisy waits, although
she does not know. A blinking light, the green
of money, beckons from her pier, aglow
like every night—I watch, though never seen.
I fill this mansion, light it up with booze
and parties, strangers shouting "more"—and come
they do, like lust to flesh, a nonstop ooze
of drunken wealth, the garish flames of Sodom.
But Daisy does not take the bait, and she's
the only one I want. I planned this all
for her. Oh, fickle love, eternal tease!
My eyes are fixed on the somber seawall,
her pallid light, only. A fortune makes
unfortunate this man, his heart, his aches.

"I think the novel is a wonder. I'm taking it home to read again and shall then write my impressions in full—but it has vitality to an extraordinary degree, and *glamour*, and a great deal of underlying thought of unusual quality. It has a kind of mystic atmosphere at times that you infused into parts of *Paradise* and have not since used. It is a marvelous fusion, into a unity of presentation, of the extraordinary incongruities of life today. And as for sheer writing, it's astonishing."

MAXWELL PERKINS

NICK
CARRAWAY

I am not even faintly like a rose
by Gary Glauber

I am not even faintly like a rose.
I wasn't even vaguely engaged.
I have been drunk just twice in my life.
I was standing beside his bed.
I was lying half asleep in the cold lower level
of the Pennsylvania Station.
I had been actually invited.
Most of the time I worked.
I felt a haunting loneliness sometimes.
I wasn't actually in love.
I felt a sort of tender curiosity.
I am one of the few honest people
that I have ever known.
I was more annoyed than interested.
I don't believe they heard a sound.
I stayed late that night.
I was reminded of something.
I wanted to get up and slap him on the back.
I was tempted to laugh whenever he opened his mouth.
I just remembered that today's my birthday.
I was feeling a little sick and
I wanted to be alone.
I walked away and left him standing there.
I couldn't sleep all night.
I didn't want to go to the city.
I thanked him for his hospitality.
I wanted to get somebody for him.
I'm five years too old to lie to myself
and call it honor.
I turned away.
I went over.
I erased it.
There was nothing I could say.
I sat there, brooding on the old unknown world.

The End of the Pier
by Linda Kraus

Nick learned that
epic success,
a life out of control
caused Jay's demise—
transitory, flawed, his financial
empire, fell—he had played his
cards poorly
the lie of an enemy
the security of old money,
Daisy's rejection of passion,
Jay's obsessive love,
a woman's unfortunate death
as well as his own.
Whether in Thebes or West Egg,
the hero falls,
but the green light at the end
of the pier still beckons.

Owl-Eyes #1
by John McCarthy

This fella is a regular Belasco,
he said to me, half-drunk

taking apart the realism
one book at a time

from the edge of a table,
his spectacles, synecdoche

to the larger one we found
our lives becoming more

illusion and wispy
with every cymbal

crashing, every lantern
blown out in the garden,

the leaves clapping
louder in their darkness

than the whole damn party
at dawn. Jordan and I

stood trapped in his gaze
watching him read

what was beyond the books,
the props, some other life,

some new depth, rearranged
by the eye's ability to expand,

choosing us and making us choose
his life or some new dream.

Saturday Night in New York
by Lewis Oakwood

Music laughter cars lights
in the moonlight
the shadowy, moving glow of
a ferryboat across the Sound.

I became aware of a new world
whispers of all human dreams
for a transitory enchanted
moment.

Nick Carraway Out in Three
by James Penha

I

Nick in Love

                              after *The Great Gatsby* chapter I

He smiled
understandingly—
he understood
and he smiled
one of those rare smiles
with a quality,
a quality of eternal,
I don't know,
reassurance in it.
He saw me; he understood me;
he reassured me that it,
that I, was
all right to have dreamed
of what might
come across once
in life. And he did.
He looked around and faced
the whole external world for an instant,
and then concentrated on me
with an irresistible prejudice
in my favor. That smile: it
understood me just as far as I dared
to be understood, believed in me
as I would like
to believe in myself,
and assured me that he had
precisely the impression that
then at least
I hoped to convey. —>

II

Nick in Heat

after *The Great Gatsby* chapter II

The elevator boy dressed soon after coming
inside Nick. "The super'll can me humming
the funeral march if he sees that 'out of order'
sign I left outside the shaft." He was drumming

his fingers on the nightstand waiting to be paid
but McKee's Leica hadn't yet been made
the receptacle of Nick's pleasure since the boy's
lever engaged eagerly, but its rapidity dismayed.

When Nick had told McKee he'd "be glad,"
he'd turned to talk directly to the lad
who'd rubbed his finger tips to deal
with McKee whose C-note was judged "not bad."

McKee promised to document the action from behind
or otherwise facelessly but Nick had to remind
the photog of his promise though the boy didn't seem to care
who was watching what as long (or short) as he could grind.

After the shot was shot and the boy had left,
McKee finally disrobed into his sheets and Nick bereft
and juxtaposed clambered out of bed and dressed
for a departure designed to be definitive if not deft.

III

Nick in Retrospect

after *The Great Gatsby* chapter IX

And as I sat there
brooding on the old,
unknown world, I thought
of my wonder when I first saw him
smile
at me who had come
to this blue lawn,
and my dream seemed
so close
that I could hardly fail to grasp it.
I did not know that it was already
behind me;
I believed in the smile,
the orgastic future
that year by year
recedes before me.
It eluded us then,
but that's no matter—
to-morrow we will run
faster,
stretch out our arms
farther...
And one fine morning—

The Letter G Confiscates the Typewriter to Assert Its POV
by Marybeth Rua-Larsen

It makes itself stick, and as Nick clicks away, abandoning Wall
Street at dusk, trying to capture the big man in words, every *g*
stroked jumps a half-inch above the line, making it a rogue
letter, the one most noticed and least understood. It won't con-
fine itself to its assigned space and tax bracket, and it won't
accept the consequences of its poor decision-making, distorting
garage, garden, champagne, dog leash and *ghosts* and prompting
some readers to draw reckless and bootlegged conclusions. Owl
glasses and a yachting cap forced low on its head don't hide it,
and like the body abandoned in the road, hit, run over, left
breast swinging, there is no remedy for random key leaps, driver
misidentification and fatal gunshot wounds. The life thought
possible, the love thought to be within reach, taunts, resulting in
a desperate *g* on an otherwise billowing curtain of prose, an
unflattering beauty mark on endless white, but the true mourner
in a mournerless room.

"And so with the sunshine and the great bursts of leaves growing on the trees, just as things grow in fast movies, I had that familiar conviction that life was beginning over again with the summer."

The Great Gatsby, Chapter I

I   feign   sleep,

as

an unbroken series of

romantic   and

abortive sorrows   .

108

Feigned Sleep
by Shloka Shankar

I feign sleep
as an unbroken series
of romantic and
abortive sorrows.

A Personality Typology from Poesy Derived
by Edward W. L. Smith

He told us that a "phrase" began to beat in his ears, the man named Nick. "There are only the pursued, the pursuing, the busy and the tired" (Fitzgerald, 1925, 1953, p. 53). More than a phrase, grammatically speaking, and perhaps an insight into a way to understand personality, typologically speaking, these few words beg exploration, if not expatiation. Unpacking this tightly wrapped laconism, sounding at once glib yet piquant, will surely give us much to ponder.

Looking first to their literary context, these words were expressed by F. Scott Fitzgerald through Nick just short of midway through *The Great Gatsby*. They came to Nick as he and Jordan Baker drove alone in Central Park, she leaning into the circle of his arm. They spoke of Daisy and of Gatsby, as they were so wont to do. From their discussion it is clear that Daisy is the pursued and that Gatsby is pursuing, though with a studied caution and more than a hint of timidity. Daisy's husband Tom had a woman on the side. He was busy. That woman, Myrtle Wilson, had a husband who was, we are told, "worn-out." Wilson was tired.

Nick was clearly enthralled by the unfolding scenario created by these four people, and particularly by the role of Gatsby. One could say that the "phrase" in question was based on empirical observations, refined in the alembic of Nick's unconscious. At least on one level, then, these characters are exemplary of the pursued, the pursuing, the busy, and the tired. But as complex characters, each in her or his way, they were more than their symbolism embraces. The fact that Nick declared, "there are *only*" (my italics) suggests that these four categories are of sufficient saliency that other aspects of character fade into the background. That is to say, the pursued, the pursuer, the busy, and the tired may be considered four personality types that for Nick's purposes said enough. Or, almost enough.

Setting this specific typology aside for now let us consider typologies per se. Psychologists sometimes speak of an *implicit personality theory*, by which they mean the propensity of people to create for themselves, a theory to explain the behavior of their fellow beings. Behavior that may seem disturbingly random, erratic, or otherwise baffling, is thereby rendered understandable, to some degree or at least less disturbing. Often such implicit personality theory is constituted at least in part by a typology. Some of these typologies hold sufficient appeal that they are admitted into the folklore and often are accompanied by a dash of humor: "There are two kinds of people in the world, those who jump into the swimming pool and those who ease in gradually." As with this example, many typologies are based on dichotomous thinking, lending them a seductive simplicity. But, this is not necessarily the case. Astrological signs make up an ancient popular typology of no less than twelve basic types, with a complex system that expands this considerably.

What in essence, then, is a psychological typology? It is an optional template that can be used to categorize behaviors, or the personal attributes that are taken as responsible for those behaviors. In order not to be overwhelmed by the complexity of human behavior, the typological template reduces the data in a manner such that they are more easily managed and comprehended. There is simplification of the data by reducing them to a limited number of categories. As is the case with popular typologies, those typologies developed by psychologists sometimes consist of dichotomies. For instance the typology based on Carl Jung's theory includes a dichotomy of *orientations*, namely *extroversion* and *introversion*, and two dichotomies of *ectopsychic functions*, those being *thinking* and *feeling* and *sensing* and *intuiting*. Note, however, that these three dichotomous dimensions may be combined into a 2 x 2 x 2 table, thus growing into a typology of eight types.

If the strength of a typology lies in its definition of a limited number of relevant categories and the perforce reduction of an overwhelming amount of data, then its weakness can be found here as well. That is to say, the act of defining certain categories at the same time defines away all other categories. Invoking the template of a typology screens out all other data as being irrelevant.

Nick was trying to understand the interpersonal dynamics of a situation that perplexed and, one might easily argue, ensorcelled him. As each of the characters assumed a role necessary to fulfill the emerging scenario, Nick saw Gatsby and Daisy clearly as the pursuer and the pursued, respectively. Given the implied polarity, a dichotomous typology is easily suggested. It seems he saw Tom and Mr. Wilson as tired and busy, respectively. In this case, however, forming a polarity is less of an obvious step. The suggestion of opposition is not inherent in the words themselves as is the case with pursuer and pursued. Could not one be tired while still busy? The key to making a dichotomy of this may lie in a temporal consideration. It seems Nick observed a chronic pattern, not just the busyness and tiredness that could coexist in particular hours or a particular day. Therefore, I suggest that the first dichotomy is the more powerful, being made up of clearer categories. The second is a weaker dichotomy given that its two terms are less clearly independent.

A further question that one may ask is whether the two dimensions of Nick's typology are independent. Although one may suggest that a person could be a busy pursuer, or a busy person being pursued, a tired pursuer, or even tired person being pursued, such convolution may do violence to the spirit of Nick's typology. No, this is neither a uni-dimensional typology with four types defined along its single dimension, nor is it a typology of two interacting dimensions that can be represented by a 2 x 2 table. It is, rather, a typology consisting of two orthogonal dimensions, each represented by two types. This can be argued strongly by the fact that Nick focused on four and only four exemplars. If this were not sufficient we need only to look once again at his wording: "There are *only*..." (my italics).

One of the dimensions of Nick's typology, pursued and pursuing can be related to what social psychologists have termed the "principle of least interest." Although of questionable grammar, this principle addresses the situation in which one person is more invested in a relationship than is the other person. As common sense would suggest, the person who has the lesser interest in the relationship is the one who tends to pursue less. The more interested person tends to be more proactive and the less interested person more passive and reactive. Various corollaries have been suggested based on this principle.

In terms of Nick's dichotomy of the busy and the tired, this suggests an inveterate dimension of psychological investigation, that of energy. At least from the time of Hippocrates, energy and activity level have been a topic of interest. Hippocrates's humoral theory identified four types: choleric (not easily inhibited, easily irritated, aggressive, expends great energy), sanguinic (energetic, easily bored, happy, friendly), phlegmatic (quiet, sluggish, slow), and melancholic (always sees the dark side, has no hope, lacks initiative). This was not only a typology descriptive of behavior, but a causal one as well. It was believed that these four types were the result of the relative amounts of yellow bile, blood, phlegm, and black bile, respectively. Although the causal agents have been replaced by a modern endocrine theory, these temperament types have been re-evoked, sometimes with name changes, even in contemporary psychology. Nick's typology reflects the behavioral aspect of this energy dimension in his naming the busy and the tired. As such, his is a descriptive typology as distinct from a causal or causal and descriptive typology.

With apology for such a pedantic description, we can say that Nick offered an empirically derived, four-type, descriptive behavior typology of two orthogonal dimensions. With these templates, he understood Daisy as the pursued, Gatsby as pursuing. Tom he saw as choleric, or in his typology, "busy." Mr. Wilson was "tired." We might say phlegmatic, bordering on melancholic.

A realist view asserts that the types are clearly visible in the world. They truly exist. In contrast, a post-modernist view avers only that a typology may be useful, regardless of objective truth. Many possible typologies thus may be equally valid. From this pragmatic perspective, one can ask whether Nick's typology is of any use. So, look about. Try out his typology. Then ask if its invocation lends you a sense of useful description, an enhanced understanding, or perhaps even predictive power. If so, give a nod to Nick. He may have shown you a way to "run faster and stretch out your arms farther."

Reference

Fitzgerald, F. S. (1925, 1953). *The Great Gatsby*. New York: Charles Scribner's Sons.

The Magician
by Susannah White

When you caught that clock
time stopped
allowing me to return
to your party tricks,
to the stories you kept spinning
like conjuring rings,
to a last garland,
a chain of white flowers—already dead
but still floating
in circles on the surface
of your green pool then
vanishing.

JORDAN BAKER

Regret
by Andrea Janelle Dickens

That afternoon, delight stretched out
stiff, half on the sidewalks and half
on the lawn. Pearls of wild rumors
demanded a word to monopolize
that night. The older girls laughed in
a hushed, fascinated way. One winter
night gay again, gay as ever. The tea-
garden girls ripped around drunk as
a monkey. That night rushed out,
pulled out the string of a cold bath
without so much as a shiver. I was
half-asleep, I was walking in
the door. I was lovely as a June
party. I was. I knew: you can hold
your tongue. You can see any little
incident. You can even see your own
careless morning: pieces of a letter,
bandages, a bottle. Careful pieces
I wanted, broken like an egg.

"[Fitzgerald is]...a dream writer...our finest novelist."

ROSS MACDONALD

MYRTLE
WILSON

Fantastic Farm
by Ed Bremson

in a valley of ashes
grotesque gardens
with transcendent powdery air

an impenetrable cloud
above the land
and spasms of paintless days

the dismal scene
with no desire in sight
a yellow wasteland

but with ash heaps
and getting off
on violence

Patience
by Sally Toner

"Thickish."

I write the word on the white board in bright purple stinky marker.

"Thickish!" I draw a line under it and turn around to face my class. Amber is texting under the table. Charles is slouched in his seat, T-shirt draped across the back of his shoulders while Betsy, his tablemate, the girl who is never without the camouflage hat I overlook even though it's against school policy, is actually paying attention. She lets the soft fabric of her black sweatshirt swallow her hands and rests her chin upon her crossed forearms. But her eyes are on me.

"THICKISH!" I shout. Now I have everyone's attention. "Isn't that the most amazing word ever?" I gush. "With one word, Fitzgerald shows us Myrtle. She's not fat. Not even dumpy. She's middle-aged, sexy (Charles raises his eyebrow) and 'thickish.'"

I explain to them that this brilliance with language is no accident. Nor was it effortless. I recite that quote from Scott to his daughter about writing: "All good writing is like swimming under water and holding your breath." These words illuminate the fear and pain the craft held for him. His letters to Scotty, while infinitely wise and clever, also expose the unremarkable quality of the language in his first drafts.

When we study Fitzgerald's life, the word patience is never the first to come to mind. He was alcoholic and fun, frenetic and spontaneous, self-destructive and hopeful. We don't envision the artisan who rewrote that sentence countless times before coming up with the word "thickish." That surgeon of syntax sitting at his desk, one pale delicate hand wrapped around a pen and the other running through his hair or rubbing his temple. That figure is unknown to most high school students who first encounter Daisy, Tom, Nick, and Jay.

I didn't understand that patience the first time I read *Gatsby*. Not even the first or second time I taught it. I found the plot contrived, the characters mawkish. This ethereal story said nothing as important as *The Grapes of Wrath*. Nothing as clever as

Catch 22. Just a pretty boy from the twenties whining about pretty people with ugly lives.

Then I read him aloud. I read aloud to my students all the time. In American lit, Patrick Henry's prose inspires, and Jonathan Edward's sermons frighten. I've always recognized the human voice as a delicate instrument, the human ear as crucial to understanding prose. So I read aloud, emphasize syllables, pause between sentences, let the alliteration and assonance roll around my tongue like butterscotch.

I imagine Fitzgerald read aloud a lot. Critics tout his visual imagery, but it's his ear that distinguishes him. I imagine his voice soft but assured, full of the Irish pride that coursed through his blood. Whatever his frailties, physical and emotional, he never doubted his work. And out of this faith came that patience we never consider. Deliberate reading, sentence after sentence, Midwestern vowels with a Princeton cadence. He reads. Nope, not right. Crosses out. Finds another word in that bottomless trough of vocabulary. Rewrites. Reads again. Nope, still not right. He makes up a word—like Dickinson.

Thickish.

I can never read the last two paragraphs of *The Great Gatsby* aloud without crying. With this class, I'll cry again. Some will smirk. Some will shift uncomfortably in their seats, half-impressed that their teacher actually loves a book so much. Do they feel that way about anything? Anyone? Benny will be ready for lunch. Betsy will go on writing her angst-ridden poetry for a couple more years, but she'll start choosing her words more carefully.

I consider patience—never my strong suit—the lesson I take, as a writer and a teacher, from Fitzgerald. Words matter. Sentences are precious and worth stepping away from, allowing them time to breathe like wine until you can come back and really understand them. Rework them until they shine with the luster they deserve.

"Fitzgerald was a better just plain writer than all of us put together."

JOHN O'HARA, in a letter to JOHN STEINBECK

LUCILLE
MC KEE

The Ripped Ball Gown
by Stefanie Lipsey

"I never care what I do, so I always have a good time. When I was here last I
tore my gown on a chair, and he asked me my name and address—and inside of
a week I got a package from Croirier's with a new evening gown in it."

(Lucille, Great Gatsby, Chapter III)

In this life, I'm a *tremolo*, excessive vibrato,
flamboyant self-indulgence
the sound of seagulls going
caw, caw, caw as they fly over your head,
screeching well past midnight,
assaulting high notes and spinning
from west egg to east,

relaxed rhythm, not too fast
are words written on the top of the score,
on the side of my boat,
in the middle of my pool,
hear the horns bellow, watch the dance floor,

she's doing the Charleston,
a ball gown's ripping on a chair,
but not for me, all I could do is discreetly toss . . .

No! I'm a *tremelo*,
a roll on one note
like the cat in the back of the orchestra says,
solid, so solid and steady as a funeral march.

Navigations
by David S. Pointer

Wrong dream celebrants—
eyes bright as yacht racing
trophies enjoying liquefied
smokeathon hovering atop
crinkled taffeta table cloth
waiting for shiny touring
cars to smoothly navigate
past the common man's
noisy embalming machine

Rambling
by Sherry Steiner

Rambling and
dancing and
singing.
Shuffling
Their feet
to the
tune of
nothing.
They care
They don't
They do
O.
Hey!
seeing
it
cut
the air
space
O place of it.
Time of
it
dancing
cha cha
cha
swinging
bringing
them home
to
light of day
light of night
O
rambling O.

"When I had finished the book, I knew that no matter what Scott did, nor how he behaved, I must know it was like a sickness and be of any help I could to him and try to be a good friend. He had many good, good friends, more than anyone I knew. But I enlisted as one more, whether I could be of any use to him or not. If he could write a book as fine as *The Great Gatsby*, I was sure he could write an even better one."

ERNEST HEMINGWAY

SCOTT & ZELDA
FITZGERALD

Oh, Zelda
by Ana Maria Caballero

Pretty much, you
were a crazy bitch.

Incensed by beauty
in others, talent in others.

No one else was Zelda.
Zelda painting. Zelda

writing. Zelda dancing.
Zelda loving. Zelda

interrupting. No one had
your husband. Or your

name. A belle,
at times, more often

a tease. Bad Zelda, who
silenced entire books.

Drunk Zelda, who shut
them down like boys.

All the rage, all of it,
yours. Sorry Zelda,

making the cottage
beds, blowing softly

at the suffering fire.
Sweet Zelda, who says

it won't be so. Again
the happy host. Again —>

the righteous muse, who,
for a second, stood right

upon the floor. But,
silly Zelda, you boiled

a pot of rings and gold,
and you got taken

to the crazy home.
The unwell woman

in the attic, with you,
told decades too late.

No new love
or worried young girl

could save you from
the locked doors above,

the savage blaze below.

To the Statue of F. Scott Fitzgerald in Rice Park,
Seen from the 53B
by Maryann Corbett

Saint Paul, Minnesota

In a December morning's stingy light,
you look, from where I sit, like one of us—
one more commuter, if a bit abstracted,
staring off to the south, the river bluffs.
It's only your intensity of stillness
that tips us off: an artwork, not a man.
That, and the fact that in subzero windchill
your head is bare. Fedora in your hand,
overcoat draped serenely on an arm,
up to the middle of your calves in snow,
snow in the crease of your Jazz Age center part,
a dapper sort of derelict, you're too
exposed for these hard times.

It looks like penance,
like something we've condemned you to, this state
of stolid dailiness, feet on the ground.
No plinth, no pedestal, no sort of height.
Just one of us again, as plain as that.
Nothing like the shine of your first great run,
you and Zelda blazing across the tabloids
looking "as though they'd stepped out of the sun."
No grander than your normal human size
in life. This makes you "accessible," we say.

But could we possibly be any crueler?
Library and theater, Hill and Ordway,
we've thrown them in your face: old family money,
the Summit greatness that you were (you said)
shut out of and obsessed with. Yes, that's us:
vindictive. We waited till they all were dead
to raise this statue—the crone who'd been your neighbor —>

and had her fill of late-night drunken shouting,
the people who recalled the White Bear Yacht Club
rooms you trashed the season before leaving
for good, sniffing that you no more belonged
here than the Riviera.
                        All the same,
you're here, because we had the final say.
Our sour old moral sense sat on your heart
all of the years you drank and binged and spent
and wrote how people send themselves to hell,
watching the glitter as it crashed away,
dying for one more story that would sell.
That made you send Nick back to the Midwest.
It stares down evil through a billboard's eye
in the book we make our children read before
—or maybe not before—they tear away.
Look at those titles: *paradise* and *damned*.
Those short stories, *atonement, benediction*...

Green light; we move. The park and Landmark Center
fade to the rear. I haul my mind from fiction
into the day's flat facts. You will remain
by the park path, kept to the straight and narrow,
eyes on the river's distance, toward *away*.
A sign of contradiction. *Ciao*. Tomorrow.

Your darling rumpled trouser
by Lois Marie Harrod

"I look down the tracks and see you coming—and out of every haze &
mist your darling rumpled trouser are hurrying to me." *Love letter from
Zelda Fitzgerald to F. Scott Fitzgerald in the first year of their marriage.*

You get the picture, they've been out all night, boozing,
Scott and Zelda, a slew of drinks, he's crocked, she's plastered,
but suddenly he's gone and she's crazy, oh god, where is he?
the way we panic when a child or lover disappears in a public place
dread blossoming in the eyes of every T. J. Eckleburg, and then
out of the railroad men's room come his darling rumpled *trouser,*
garment larking back to the Irish quip, *A jellous wife*
is like an Irish trouze, alwayes close to her mans tayle,
no *r*'s yet, no *s*, a *carouse* of a word with no consequence,
his *trouser,* the singularity saucing down the tracks, one pant
with two legs glazing the Gaelic, banshee-shamrock,
bombed and blitzed, the *darling rumpled trouser,* the legs of him, hers,
rumpled from whatever stumbles a *trouser, wed, bed,* the dog
who slept in his skin, old Bowser, slosh of trouser, slosh of gin
and a smile as wide as the track on his puss, no history yet,
no idea where this tanked train is going, no green light
to mark the end of the dock.

Even the Great Author Doubts His Merit
by Joanie Hieger Fritz Zosike
Sept. 2, 2014, NYC

The Great Gatsby.
What's so great about him?
What's so great about it?

I'd have rather it'd been called
Trimalchio on West Egg,
Conferring a pretention it merits,

Better yet, *The High Bouncing Lover,*
All the better to bounce you with,
My dear. My dear Gatsby. Gatz,

For short. And was he short?
Did he fall short? A shortfall? What?
Got caught with his shorts down? Hot!

The trials and tribulations of the rich
And self-obsessed, the self-professed
Elite, wrapped in their classist, racist

Sheets of satin, oblivious to the flask
In the garter of a honky-tonk tramp,
Distant cousin of her high-falutin'

Disco ball aunt on the Island, Egg
About to break. Why do we even care?
While poor F. Scott died doubting

That this masterpiece held sway
He felt compelled to tell the story
Of his day, and his quiet disillusion.

Hallowed Books
by Shahé Mankerian

Never trust a man who reads before sleep;
he snoozes through revolutions like Van Winkle.

If a woman removes jackets from books,
she must be concealing big, green warts

underneath her corset. Do not press flowers
or butterflies between pages of the Bible;

they're not bookmarks, and you're not Nabakov.
A fireman hid 30 shekels in a hollowed book.

God burned him in a furnace at 451° Fahrenheit.
Gatsby wanted to use gilded books as doorstops;

F. Scott made him stare at East Egg instead.
In New York, I bought roasted peanuts once

wrapped in a ripped page from *Naked Lunch*.

Once Again, To Zelda
by Christina M. Rau

So we beat on,
boats against the current,
borne back ceaselessly
into the past.

Boats against the current,
into the past,
the green light glows
through the mist.

Into the past,
through the mist,
it was an hour of profound
human change.

Through the mist
human change
and excitement
on the air.

Human change
on the air
parceled out at birth
material without being real.

On the air
material without being real
is the thing you never
deeply blame a woman for.

Material without being real:
deeply blame a woman for
a new world,
the orgastic future.

Deeply blame a woman for
the orgastic future,
too old to lie
and call it honor.

The orgastic future,
too old to lie
where the dark fields of the republic
rolled on under the night.

Too old to lie,
rolled on under the night,
it eludes us into
the unquiet darkness.

The Roaring Twenties
by Marianne Titirigia & Matthew Oldham Smith

INT. THE SPEAKEASY – NIGHT

Festive and smoke-filled, the club roars with excitement. Twenty-something WOMEN dressed as Flappers fill the dance floor, coupled with twenty-something MEN in 1920s attire.

RONNI (24), a quirky beauty, joins MIRANDA (25) on the bar. They dance, valiantly bumping hips and shaking chests. It's a deviant Charleston.

ZACK and SCOTT (25), dressed in 1920s suits, enter from the side street.

MIRANDA/RONNI
Scott!/Scott?

Zack walks over. Surprise!

ZACK/SCOTT
Happy Birthday, Miranda.

Miranda jumps into Scott's arms, followed by Ronni into Zack's. Miranda hugs Scott before letting go. They take in the moment.

MIRANDA
I can't believe you're here. I'm speechless.

ZACK
That's a first.

Zack and Ronni snap photos with their phones.

MIRANDA
This is the best gift of the night.

142

                        ZACK
        Icing on the Miranda-quarter-of-a-century-old cake.

Ronni grabs a cigarette. Scott lights it with his Zippo.

                        RONNI
            So suave

                        MIRANDA
            Yeah, who knew those fingers had talents beyond
            typing . . .

Scott hands Miranda a gift.

                        SCOTT
            Take this before I reconsider.

Zack takes a drag off of Ronni's cigarette. He links arms with
Ronni. They walk off.
                        MIRANDA
            Scott, you didn't have to come.

Scott takes a deep breath. He scans the room.

                        SCOTT
            The past is the past. I came tonight because for
            once, I want to be there for you.

He motions to her gift. Miranda unwraps it. It's a book titled,
Dawn of a New Era.
                        SCOTT
            It's the very first copy. Look.

Scott takes the book and turns to page three. He hands it back.

                        SCOTT
            I dedicated it to you.

                    MIRANDA
          I don't know what to say.

                     SCOTT
          Good, don't say anything, because I was wondering,
          you know, now that I've spilled my guts, and the
          book is done, if you would...

                    MIRANDA
          Scott, we're friends now. We can't mess with that
          again.

                     SCOTT
          Oh, I know, trust me. I wanted to ask if you'd be
          interested in planning the release party. I was
          thinking about recommending you to my new
          publicist.

                    MIRANDA
          Are you serious? I'd love to! I need a real job.

The MUSIC cuts out. Zack and Ronni walk over holding a cake,
candles aflame, singing "Happy Birthday." Scott joins in, followed by surrounding GUESTS. Zack spots DIANE waving at him
from across the room. He hides behind the cake. The song ends.

                     ZACK
          Make a wish.

He shoves the cake toward Miranda. She closes her eyes as Zack
ducks behind Scott, almost dropping the cake. Scott saves it.

                ZACK (CONT'D)
                  (to Scott)
          Jesus, what the hell is Diane doing here?

Miranda opens her eyes and blows out the candles. Zack maneu-
vers around Ronni. Diane approaches.

                    DIANE
        I've been looking all over for you.

                    ZACK
        Diane! What are you doing here?

                    DIANE
        I saw your Facebook check in, silly.

                    ZACK
        That was like, five minutes ago.

                    DIANE
        I was hanging out with some friends down the
        street. Don't worry, I'm not stalking you or
        anything.

She leans in for a kiss. Zack offers his cheek. Miranda and
Ronni are perplexed. Behind her, Scott motions that she's crazy.
He whispers in Zack's ear.

                    SCOTT
        Foiled by Facebook, again.

Zack swoops Diane away before any introduction.

                    ZACK
        Let's grab that booth. Those shoes must be
        killing you.

Nick approaches from behind the bar.

                    NICK
        Scott? Hey, man, I didn't know you were coming.
        What can I get you?

                    SCOTT
        Uh, club soda. Thanks.

Zack rejoins them, downing the rest of his martini.

ZACK
I'll have another.

NICK
Manners, my friend. Ladies first.

He walks over to Ronni.

NICK (CONT'D)
What can I get you besides this?

He kisses Ronni. Zack sticks his finger down his throat.

RONNI
I'll have a water.

MIRANDA
Me too.

NICK
(to Ronni)
Water? Judging from those moves a little while ago,
I thought you'd want something a little harder.

MIRANDA
Calm down, Casanova, she's not looking for a stiff
one right now.

RONNI
But maybe later.

MIRANDA
And you say I'm the slut.

RONNI
You are. How many guys have sexted, I mean
texted, you tonight?

                    MIRANDA
          Guys are like shoes. A girl needs options.

                    NICK
          I'm gonna get the drinks.

                    SCOTT
          Hold on, Nick.

Scott turns to Miranda and Ronni.

                    SCOTT (CONT'D)
          I'd rather not be here if you feel like you have to
          change around me.

Miranda and Ronni look at each other, then Nick.

                    MIRANDA/RONNI
          I'll have a martini./The usual.

                    NICK
          Got it.

Nick walks off. Suddenly, a SIREN wails. Red lights FLASH
from outside.

The music cuts out as three buff COPS walk into the bar. Diane
panics and sneaks out the back door.

                    COP #1
          We got a call about some unlawful activity going on
          down here. Smoking is not permitted inside the
          premises. Who's responsible for this?

                    MIRANDA
          What is this? A Prohibition prank?

Miranda continues to smoke, defiantly.

ZACK
Miranda, put it out!

Miranda walks toward the cop with drunken confidence.

MIRANDA
I know we're smoking, but it's a private party. And
it's my birthday. Please don't ruin it over a few little
puffs of smoke.

COP #1
It's your birthday, is it? Well then, you've been a
very bad girl. Take her away, men.

The Ballet Dancer
by Matthew Wilson

Scott rattled on his typewriter, to ease his loneliness from Zelda's madness
Yet is remembered as a father to his, not her golden-haired child
The maker of Gatsby who took the blame and fall for such a crime
As petty as the wrong target for a hardhearted man's hate.

Zelda—this little ballerina—was jealous of the love Scott had for his son
And danced into the arms of others to make him look up from work
Love in the real world is brief and Scott wished to give the world
A hero that they would love for all eternity, safe from Zelda's spite.

This flapper, dancing by the window to the melody of his typewriter keys
That Gatsby lived at all is a miracle for her interruptions in his making
This wanton destruction to stillbirth the chance of a character to overshade her
And let history speak of the short-lived children, rather the lonely wife.

"[Fitzgerald] had one of the rarest qualities in all literature, and it's a great shame that the word for it has been thoroughly debased by the cosmetic racketeers, so that one is almost ashamed to use it to describe a real distinction. Nevertheless, the word is charm—charm as Keats would have used it...It's not a matter of pretty writing or clear style. It's a kind of subdued magic, controlled and exquisite, the sort of thing you get from good string quartettes.

RAYMOND CHANDLER

FURTHERMORE

Green, Blue, and Yellow:

The use of colors as adjectives in The Great Gatsby

by Anthony Costello

Gold

Perhaps surprisingly, given the gaudy party scenes at Jay Gatsby's West Egg mansion, and the frequent mention of finance— money, bonds, stocks and securities—"gold" as an adjective is only mentioned three times in the novel, and two of those in the epigraph...

> Then wear the gold hat, if that will move her;
> if you can bounce high, bounce for her two,
> Till she cry "Lover, gold-hatted, high-bouncing lover,
> I must have you"' —Thomas Parke d'Invilliers

...and once to describe Gatsby wearing "a gold-colored tie."

Silver

Used wistfully to describe Gatsby "standing with his hands in his pockets regarding the silver pepper of the stars" and once to describe his "silver shirt."

The Great Gatsby is a claustrophobic novel. Perhaps this little sprinkle of silver dilutes the cocksure display of bolder colors. Gatsby looking at the stars allows brief respite from the noisy, stifling drama of the novel?

Pink

The jacket to my Penguin Classics edition (2006) of *The Great Gatsby* is a soft pink; the color is used only three times. Twice in adjacent chapters, albeit movingly and pertinently, where pink links Jay Gatsby and Daisy Buchanan. In the chapters following Myrtle Wilson's death, Nick Carraway describes Gatsby as wearing a "gorgeous pink rag of a suit" and notices "the pink glow from Daisy's room" at her mansion in East Egg. Pink is silence. Pink is loneliness. Both Daisy and Gatsby are alone and silent at the moment of the narrator's description. Famously, in chapter five, Daisy says to Gatsby that she would "like to get one of those pink clouds and put you in it and push you around." Pink is wishing and a wistful unrequitedness.

Grey

Grey leads to yellow, or yellow leads to grey. Nick Carraway describes Jordan Baker as washed-out: "Her grey sun-streaked eyes looked back at me." On his first meeting with Gatsby: "We talk about some wet, grey little village in France." Clouds are "small, grey clouds." "Grey cars crawl" along the "grey land" between West Egg and New York. In a city ensemble piece there is "a grey (scrawny) Italian child" and an "old grey man" sells the puppy dog to Tom Buchanan. "Grey windows" give way to illuminated light at Gatsby's extravagant parties. If the aftermath of the First World War is grey, then it is perhaps foretold that grey will also follow the yellowing drama of the Roaring Twenties, the 1929 stock market crash occurring four years after the publication of Fitzgerald's novel. Eight greys.

Red

Red is versatile. Red (including crimson) stands out at a distance. No more so than in the beautiful and deceptively simple description of the landscape between Long Island and New York: "where new red petrol pumps sat out in pools of light." This image prefigures the America represented in the paintings of Edward Hopper. Red is used in description of character: Colleen, Myrtle Wilson's sister, is portrayed as "a slender working girl of about thirty with a solid sticky bob of red hair..."; and place: "the crimson room bloomed with light." Red is used for the fourth time (dramatically) as the outline of the mattress Gatsby was lounging on before he was murdered: "a thin red circle in the water."

Green

A color of omniscient significance for the author. In one of the most revealing statements about his hero, Fitzgerald utilizes green thus: "Gatsby believed in the green light, the orgastic future that year by year recedes before us." This quote is a leitmotif for the novel. The use of green is striking and difficult to comprehend. Not green manifesting as envy, or naivety; nothing to do with the environment or protean growth. But green suggesting sex and recrudescence? Today, the Green Card suggests a future in the United States for the recipient; for Fitzgerald, green is something of an oxymoron...the receding future. Placed at the end of the book, the quote reminds us of the two occasions where the word was used previously. Nick Carraway tells us: "I thought of Gatsby's wonder when he first picked out the green light at the end of Daisy's dock." And Gatsby to Daisy: "You always have a green light that burns all night at the end of your dock." Daisy tells Nick to present "a green card" if he wants to kiss her. Daisy "giving out green..." Gatsby's car has a "green leather seat" and the stretch of water between East and West Egg is "the green sound." Green is magma, undercurrent, centrifugal momentum, the mysterious life and death force running with subtle menace through the novel. Used six times.

White

White is used on thirteen occasions. It is used to describe minor characters, some introduced by name only. Mr McKee (from the flat below, but attending Myrtle Wilson's infamous New York gathering) is described as having a "white spot of lather on his cheekbone" and never mentioned again. Nick Carraway describes himself and Gatsby matter-of-factly as "wearing a white flannel suit'" there is a "white plum tree" and Myrtle Wilson wears "a cream-colored chiffon." Colleen's face, in the same description of her detailed in red, is powdery "white." There are "white steps" up to Gatsby's mansion; we see "white moonlight" and "white banners." Like the color itself, these usages fade into the background. Perhaps this is why white is often thought of as a non-color. But white is used to suggest innocence and purity when Daisy reminisces about hers and Jordan Baker's adolescence: our "white girlhood." There is also a sepulchral description of George Wilson. In shock at Myrtle's death and the seeds of revenge sown "a white ashen dust veiled his dark suit."

Black

Black appears once in the novel, perhaps anti-Semitically, to describe a "Jewess with black hostile eyes."

Blue

Blue is used as an adjective ten times. This color casts a series of atmospheric shadows throughout the book. Without this use of blue *The Great Gatsby* would be an inferior novel. Blue gives the book a blue tone, blue moods, blue atmosphere, blue delights. Blue tends to permeate more than any other color. It seeps through the surrounding pages. Blue is a long-term investment for the author's ambition in this novel. If yellow is the plotting and characterization, then blue is its structure and style. Cast in a blue light, the novel resembles something like a fable or a fairytale. Describing the grounds of Gatsby's mansion and the people coming and going Fitzgerald writes this humdinger of perfect prose: "In his blue gardens men and girls came and went like moths among the whisperings and the champagne and the stars." Blue is the color that Nick Carraway associates with Gatsby as a self-made man: "He had come a long way to this blue lawn." The novel moves through the "blue smoke of brittle leaves." The dress of Lucille, an uninvited guest at one of Gatsby's nightly parties is "gas-blue," a chauffeur's uniform is "robin's egg blue." About Myrtle: "a streak of hair lay like a dash of blue paint across her cheek." Gatsby has an (Indian) blue shirt, a character has "a blue nose," George Wilson has "light-blue eyes." The pivotal part of the plotline before the climax of the novel revolves around misunderstanding about the color of two cars. Tom Buchanan's is a blue coupe."

Yellow

And Gatsby's car is yellow. There are ten adjectival yellows in *The Great Gatsby*. Yellow is the color of decay, the color of the dark side of the American dream, but also the color of locomotives! Delving into the past of the narrator, Fitzgerald writes of "murky yellow cars of the Chicago, Milwaukee, and St Paul Railroad." The approach to George Wilson's garage where "The only building in sight was a small block of yellow brick." Yellow is the end of summer. Jordan Baker has "autumn-leaf yellow in her hair." The soulless and decadent picture of a city that never sleeps at Tom and Myrtle's party in New York. Nick Carraway mentions that "big over the city our line of yellow windows." At

Gatsby's parties, symbolizing an increasing level of decadence and meaninglessness, "the orchestra is playing yellow cocktail music." Two girls at Gatsby's parties are wearing "twin yellow dresses." Yellow is decay and shallowness. The fetishizing of the (yellow) automobile. The motor car as status symbol. Why is Jay Gatsby's car yellow? Because in the way that F. Scott Fitzgerald appropriates yellow elsewhere it is the perfect and logical color in which to tempt fate through accidental slaughter? Yellow had been increasing in speed and intensity throughout the novel. After Myrtle is killed by Gatsby's yellow car (with Daisy at the wheel, it is implied by Gatsby, but never corroborated), the police are investigating the local protagonists and the color yellow is on the lips of characters and in the ears of readers.

"It was a yellow car."

"Big yellow car."

The negro "began to talk about a yellow car."

And again..."it was a yellow car."

George Wilson "has a way of finding out who owns the yellow car."

Providence abounds in yellow. Fitzgerald could have chosen a dozen other colors for Jay Gatsby's car. As author, Fitzgerald knew of Gatsby's fate, and allows us to believe, with the solemn rituals of his preparation for bathing in his swimming pool, that Gatsby himself knew. Nick Carraway's last description of Gatsby is "and in a moment disappeared among the yellowing trees." Ten yellows.

Green, blue and yellow are the novel's primary colors. Blue and yellow interplay throughout *The Great Gatsby*. Blue sets the tone; yellow forces the action. Yellow foretells death and is symbolic of decay; blue gives a sense of lustrous security in the myth of its own promise. If yellow is ugly, blue is often beautiful; if blue is mysterious, yellow is more honest. Blue and yellow are not opposites. They complement each other as they do on the color wheel. The magic is that ten yellows and ten blues in the hands of Fitzgerald stretch across the entire canvas of his great novel. The strange use of adjectival green, the meaning of green, underpinning everything. And, of course, the other colors mentioned have their part to play, too.

The Last Page
by David M. Katz

O soften West Egg to a hush,
Steal what you will from nineteen-twenty
And that island near the heaped-up ash
Hard by the dark road from the city!
You'll leave it spare of nervous speech
And money, pure of all save Daisy.
Guilty, she strolls his painful beach,
His shoreline spawn of rotting beauty.
Style, Scott, it's style you've sent to cleanse
Dutch sailors' eyes, swung back to see
Their vanished trees—that virgin lens
You've lent to catch the breath of Gatsby.

Green Light
by LynleyShimat Lys

The little green light blinks
and the avatar appears of a man at prayer
in the city he isn't living in. And I want
to say hi, shabbat shalom, but I'm afraid
he's going to think I want to remind him
of a favor he's promised me. And that's not
what I want him to think about. So I try to post
something clever, something smart, an avenue
to conversation. But goats, leaping goats
are all I've got. Video of goats in someone's
living room, leaping and clacking
across the floor and on the couches.
And the little green light disappears.
And I wait and hold my breath and
watch the baby goats. And I wish he
would post something, I wish I could
tease him about wearing coats and
how the cold there has him
in fleece hats. I wish—
But this time I'm
leaving, the green lights
will shift time zones.
And I'll feel once again
that Jerusalem is the center of the world
and I am not there. And the light
blinks on again, he's here, but not posting,
not commenting. No opening. No text
And the light disappears. And I'm full of jokes
and goats again. And I know
he has things to ask me, I want to open him
so the words spill out. I want the words
to roll off our tongues and leap
around the room and bounce off tables and chairs.

The Destruction of Desire
by Suzanne Rawlinson

The telephone, startlingly.
All subjects, vanished into air.
Candles lit, pointlessly.
Instinct immediately for the police.
A vigil beside a tangible body.
Daisy chain of connecting verandas,
Music from my neighbor, moths among the whispering stars.
Diving from the raft, taking the sun, cataracts of foam.
A bar, real brass Oboes, trombones, saxophones and drums.

Chatter, laughter, forgotten on the spot,
New arrivals dissolve, confident, sharp,
One, guest actually invited.
The honor would be entirely Gatsby's.
Rules of behavior; simplicity of heart, ticket of admission,
Well-dressed, a little hungry, solid, prosperous.
My host: denied, purposeless and alone.
New York: racy, adventurous, restless
Fifth Avenue women disapprove and smiled warm darkness.
Metropolitan twilight, a haunting loneliness, poignant moments
"He killed a man"
What's your opinion of me, anyhow?
That house just across the bay.
We've met before, a laugh.
This moment, dangerously turned, trembling rigidly.
Bewilderment faint, doubt to the present happiness.
Vitality of illusion. It had gone beyond everything.
Passion bright, drifted fire, freshness challenge,
A rush of emotion, fluctuating warmth,
They had forgotten me.

Penniless without a past, invisible,
ravenously unscrupulous one night,
took the right to touch. Under false phantom,
deliberately given security; from the same stratum

The shots: anxious, alarmed, scarcely a word said,
Movement of the water toward the drain
Ripples moved irregularly down the pool.
A thin red circle in the water.
"You're worth the whole damn bunch"
The only compliment from beginning to end.
"Goodbye, old sport."

Words for The Great Gatsby
by Lee Upton

Tom's first words: "I've got a nice place here."
Daisy's: "I'm p-paralysed with happiness."
Jordan Baker's: "Absolutely."
Gatsby's: "Your face is familiar."

Tom's last words: "By God it was awful—"
Jordan Baker's: "I thought it was your secret pride."
Daisy's: "I can't stand this any more."
Gatsby's: "Well, good-bye."

Myrtle Wilson is Gatsby with even less luck.
Her first words: "Get some chairs, why don't you,
so somebody can sit down."
Owl Eyes's last words: "The poor son-of-a-bitch."

Gatsby's first words that Nick hears when Daisy's at his house:
"We've met before." Then "I'm sorry about the clock."
Every word counts. Even
Gatsby's boyhood book *Hopalong Cassidy*.

Its first sentence
contains this phrase:
"so many dead of daring
which verged on the insane."

To Look Up and Remember
Found poem from underlined copy of The Great Gatsby
purchased at thrift store for $1
by Melanie Villines

plagiaristic
abortive
superficial
proximity
supercilious
uninflected
and
I tumbled with a sort
of splash upon the keys of a ghostly piano.
Her
porch was bright with the bought luxury of star-shine:
The
shadow of a tree fell abruptly across the dew and
ghostly birds began to sing among the blue leaves.
There was a slow, pleasant movement in the air,
scarcely a wind, promising a cool, lovely day
them clustered open-mouthed
grotesque
circumstantial, eager, and untrue.
When Michaelis's
testimony at the inquest brought to light. Wilson's sus-

They Slipped Briskly into an Intimacy from Which
They Never Recovered
by Amy Schreibman Walter

with the sunshine and the great bursts of leaves growing on the trees
just as things grow in fast movies. *I won't kiss you.*
It might get to be a habit and I can't get rid of habits.

She wanted for a moment to hold
and devour him, wanted his mouth, his ears; his coat collar

The sentimental person thinks things will last

I don't care about truth. I just want some happiness
Lie to me by the moonlight. Do a fabulous story.

My God; you're fun to kiss.
Her heart sank into her shoes.
It takes two to make an accident.

So we'll just let things take their course, and never be sorry
Think how you love me. I ask you to remember. There will always be
the person I am tonight.

The afternoon made them tranquil for a while
as if to give them a deep memory for the long parting
the next day promised

Well, let it pass,
April is over
April is over

And so we beat on
angry, and half in love
she wouldn't let go
of the letter. She took it into the tub
and squeezed it up in a wet ball; it was coming to pieces

like snow.
In two weeks it'll be the longest day in the year

And so we beat on
with the sunshine and the great bursts
of leaves growing on the trees

NOTES FROM THE AUTHORS

KATIE ALIFERIS (Daisy): *The Great Gatsby* is one of my favorite books and I read it (usually) yearly. Rarely does a story produce so much emotion while maintaining the floral eloquence found in F. Scott Fitzgerald's words. My poem is inspired by the desperate, life-shattering desire Gatsby feels for Daisy.

E. KRISTIN ANDERSON (Unpleasantness this Afternoon): The poem is an erasure based on the Scribner paperback edition (2004), pages 144-145, where after the car accident Nick finds Gatsby in the dark outside Daisy's house watching her windows.

MARIA IVANA TREVISANI BACH (The Great Gatsby's Dream): I was inspired by the last words of *The Great Gatsby*. "So we beat on, boats against the current, borne back ceaselessly into the past." Because seldom do we realize the Great Dream of ours!

JOHANNES S.H. BJERG (slip it on): Erasure poem taken from page 35.

JULIE E. BLOEMEKE (Telephone): While studying *The Great Gatsby*—I was fortunate enough to have done graduate work with Fitzgerald biographer Matthew J. Bruccoli at the University of South Carolina—I became fascinated by Fitzgerald's use of the telephone as a presence in conversation. The mystery of who is on the other end of the wire lends resonance to Gatsby's intrigue; the insistence of Fitzgerald's *shrill metallic urgency* is often used to punctuate, disrupt, pause, or hijack. My current poetry manuscript—largely influenced by our deepening connection to the cell phone—offers a grateful hat tip to Fitzgerald's adroit observations of the telephone's importance in social dynamics.

ED BREMSON (Fantastic Farm): A found poem from Chapter II of *The Great Gatsby*.

ANA MARIA CABALLERO (Oh, Zelda): After Hemingway's *A Moveable Feast*.

SAM CHA (C A R V): Erasure (but with punctuation that's mostly mine) from Chapter V of *The Great Gatsby*—the familiar Scribner reissue paperback edition from 2004.

JAN CHRONISTER (Genesis): Found poem from The Great Gatsby Scribner paperback edition 2004.

HELEN DALLAS (An Oxford Girl): "An Oxford Girl" is a fictionalized memoir of my struggle with depression. Fitzgerald's writings have considerably impacted my style of writing and have also been integral to my recovery. From him, I learned that the golden times in the past are more toxic on examination. It was for myself that I learned it gets better. I hope I have done justice to the work that did so much for me.

TRACY DAVIDSON (Valley of Ashes): I looked online for some notable quotes from the book for inspiration. When I started reading them, quite a number of phrases jumped out at me as being very suitable for tanka poems (in the traditional, and now rarely seen, 5-7-5-7-7 syllable format). I started playing around with them, taking a snatch of text here and mixing it with another snatch there. Eventually I came up with this eight-verse tanka sequence. Every single word is F Scott Fitzgerald's—just jumbled up by me!

SUSAN DE SOLA (Little Naomi): Arnold Rothstein, the model for Wolfsheim, bore no physical resemblance to the anti-Semitic caricature in either Fitzgerald's novel (1922) or Luhrmann's film (2013).

ANDREA JANELLE DICKENS: (Regret) For this poem, I used just the dialogue of Jordan Baker as my source text. I was intrigued by how enigmatic her character seems at times, and how clear it seems at other times, and used this as a starting point for playing with found phrases.

JENNIFER FINSTROM (Almost Sonnet Written While Thinking About First Love, Greek Mythology, and *The Great Gatsby*): This poem is a part of a series of "Almost Sonnets" that I'm working on, and one of the constraints that I've created for writing them is that the poem should include a quote from the work it is in conversation with—in this case, of course, *The Great Gatsby*. Another element specific to this series is that of nostalgia, which also works well with Fitzgerald's novel.

JEANNINE HALL GAILEY (Heroines at 40: Daisy Buchanan): Fitzgerald's *The Great Gatsby* was a much-loved and reread book when I was young and was maybe the first time I noticed and was influenced by a writer's style, sentence structure, and imagery. I think I memorized a few paragraphs when was eleven or twelve. I always wanted Daisy to be given more of a character, more of a voice, and this poem is my attempt to do that.

SHIVAPRIYA GANAPATHY (Unheard Melodies): My erasure poem was created from the first chapter of the novel.

MARIELLE GAUTHIER (Tortured Hands): The romance, the wealth, and the pain it brought Gatsby all aided my thought process in writing this poem.

GARY GLAUBER (I am not even faintly like a rose): First published online at *Verbatim Poetry*. All lines are taken (in chronological order) from F. Scott Fitzgerald's *The Great Gatsby*, 75th *anniversary edition*.

SENNA HEYATAWIN (erasure etude: variation 2): I heard about the anthology submission through a discussion I had the good fortune to overhear...and how I love F. Scott Fitzgerald, and all of his books. So I thank you for the opportunity to practice erasure on a wonderful piece of literature like *The Great Gatsby*. I took an excerpt from Chapter III of the book, and wrote the first erasure on the piece...leaving blanks, and guesstimating the spacing as close to the paragraph as written in the novel page. I like the text showing dimly behind the poem but still don't know that technique yet for my poems. With this work, I liked how the variations developed in the space and line design offered by using the text as written. F. Scott Fitzgerald was such a master.

JOANIE HIEGER FRITZ ZOSIKE (Even the Great Author Doubts His Merit): I'd always had a bone to pick with *The Great Gatsby*; not with the writing itself, but with the cultural segment it depicts. As with soap opera, it explores "the trials and tribulations of the rich and shameless" (as my brother Bobby calls it), a subject that holds little sway for me. But that's my prejudice. What interests me most about *The Great Gatsby* is the backstory of Fitzgerald's self-doubt about his work and, ultimately, even his own merit as a human being. According to biographical information, I glean that Fitzgerald became what he held up to a critical light. And it is perhaps those flaws and his vulnerability that prompted me to write this poem. I attempt with it to crack open the Egg. And as for Zelda, well, she's another story altogether!

SHAWN P. HOSKING (Perfect): I started with a quote from Fitzgerald, "I love her and that is the beginning of everything." Of course, the book ends in tragedy, but he never stops reaching for her. Even in that last second of his life. He looks across the bay and reaches for her. Refusing to give up his image of her. In my poem, that's all he wants—to see his perfect Daisy. He changed himself to win her back, hence the gilded man. But he never seems to accept that there are things that you can't change. If he can just keep the light in sight he can keep his dream real, but his dream, the light, fades along with his eyesight.

VERONICA HOSKING (Infamous Crush): I was introduced to the double dactyl poetry form a couple years ago, and I'm still working hard at perfecting its rhythm and rhyme.

MATHIAS JANSSON (Past): The poem is based on a dialogue in the novel: "I wouldn't ask too much of her," I ventured. "You can't repeat the past." "Can't repeat the past?" he cried incredulously. "Why of course you can!" The text is repeated in the background and in the foreground you see an image of USA with a tag cloud created with help of all the paragraphs in the novel containing the word past.

JEN CULLERTON JOHNSON (The Gatsby Man): I lived and worked in Japan for two years in the small town mentioned in my piece. The essay is part of a larger work called *Yoshimura's Ghost: One Year in Rural Japan*.

DAVID M. KATZ (The Last Page): My poem is an offshoot of a terrific exercise the poet David Yezzi assigned in a prosody workshop he taught about a decade ago. David told us to select a portion of that memorable last page of *Gatsby* and render that passage into blank verse. I found that it wasn't all that difficult to render Fitzgerald's rhythmic prose into verse, a task that further revealed to me the lucidity and power of Scott's style. And it's that style I pay homage to in my poem—a style that revealed the spirit and energy of a most remarkable era in American life.

LAURIE KOLP (Tea with a Tiger): Found poem, *The Great Gatsby* (Scribner, 2004) p. 66 & 67.

LINDA KRAUS (The End of the Pier): Gatsby's tortuous quest for love became a kind of totem for me over the years; I wished to honor its significance in my own life as well as in the lives of many generations of readers by writing this poem.

SAMANTHA LEVAN (Formality on Scalloped White Wings): Erasure on *The Great Gatsby* (Scribner Trade Paperback Edition, 2004), pages 56, 57, and 125.

CAOLAN MADDEN (Discover the Story Behind These Luxurious Pearls): In spring 2013, members of a women's poetry group I belong to decided to see the Gatsby movie together, and that we should probably reread the novel in preparation. This poem is a pretty faithful record of two days of Gatsby rereading—including my surprise at Daisy's nastiness, a minor car accident and subsequent visit to the obstetrician (I was pregnant with my first child, a daughter), and some bizarre and sometimes offensive emails I got from Tiffany advertising *The Great Gatsby* jewelry collection. The poem starts with Chapter III and ends, at bedtime, midway through Chapter VII. I did end up seeing the movie with my poet friends—you can read Becca Klaver's poem in this anthology to see how that went, or you can read our collaborative play, *Girl Talk Triptych*! But even though many secrets were revealed to me about Gatsby's past, I somehow managed not to discover the story behind those luxurious pearls.

MARJORIE MANWARING (Thinking About Someone I Used To Love): Previously published in *Search for a Velvet-lined Cape* by Marjorie Manwaring (Mayapple Press) and *Fire On Her Tongue: An eBook Anthology of Contemporary Women's Poetry* (Two Sylvias Press).

GEORGE MCKIM (the lawns): Erasure poem from Chapter IV with original painting.

CHRISTINA MURPHY (Ascend into Dreams): My creative process in writing this poem was an effort to imagine what a vision of the highest freedom of ascending into dreams would be like for a man of Jay Gatsby's intense imagination and romantic sensibilities. I have always

170

been mesmerized by the intensity of Gatsby's imagination and ability to envision his own created and idealized world. And so I sought for this poem the types of images and conceptual frameworks that would best exemplify what the passion and the intensity of Gatsby's vision of love would be like. That concept guided me through the drafts of this poem until I felt it captured the idea and ideal of Gatsby as the consummate dreamer for whom creating and sustaining his romantic vision became his life's passion.

LESLIE NICHOLS (Eat Gatsby): These erasure poems are created from the 1995 Scribner Paperback edition: "supper" is composed with text from pages 21 and 139; "second supper" is created from pages 6-7 and 47-49. The first role of the brackets is to reference the text erased in the process of creating the poem. I hope they do other work such as creating a sense of density and confinement in the "second supper." Brackets used in a related way appear in the scholar Anne Carson's translation of Sappho's fragments called "If Not, Winter." I first saw them used in erasure poetry to reference the absence of text in poet Kristina Marie Darling's collection *Petrarchan* "Appendix B: Misc. Fragments."

LEWIS OAKWOOD (A Saturday Night in New York): An erasure poem taken from the novel's final page.

ALYSSON B. PARKER (Standing on Daisy's Dock): I have always been enamored with the Roaring Twenties, as my parents collected antique cars. One was a beige Studebaker, which I always imagined could have been tooling around with Jay Gatsby in the area of West Egg. As a high school English teacher, I've taught *Gatsby* from a Humanities perspective—music and dance included—and I am never disappointed with how my students delight in the novel.

PATRICK T. REARDON (Inside): My erasure poem is based on page 71 of the Crown Classics edition (Harper Press, London 2012).

CHRISTINA M. RAU (Once Again, To Zelda): After years of reading *The Great Gatsby* over and again, and then teaching parts of it here and there, the underlined passages and marginalia have taken over my only copy, and I refuse to get a new one even though this one is pretty overused and beaten up. That's how I like my books. In thinking about honoring this book, my favorite for many reasons, I couldn't find my own words to do it justice. And so, I pored through the pages, copying all the underlined passages. Then I found which lines worked the best with others. Then I focused on rhythm, squaring up quatrains in a neat sequence to retell the essence of Gatsby. The repetition of each strategically chosen quote builds a tone that should mimic the tone by the end of the novel.

SUZANNE RAWLINSON (The Destruction of Desire): The majority of the poem was constructed through the erasure method. I went through the text picking parts that stuck out in my mind. Then using those blocks of text, I omitted parts to capture the feeling I wanted. Two parts of the poem were constructed through the found poetry method—this was where speech was used. (Collins Classics, *The Great Gatsby*, Edition published in 2013.)

SHLOKA SHANKAR (Feigned Sleep): My poem is an erasure culled from Chapter I of *The Great Gatsby*. The artwork and effects were added digitally using an online photo editor.

MARIANNE TITIRIGA AND MATTHEW OLDHAM SMITH (The Roaring Twenties): This is the opening scene from our screenplay *The Roaring Twenties*. The script explores the notion of history repeating itself, and centers on a group of twenty-something friends living what appears to be the high life in modern-day Manhattan. Like the characters F. Scott Fitzgerald explored in *The Great Gatsby*, our characters discover that reckless ways have consequences—both personally and professionally.

SALLY TONER (Patience): This essay took first place in the creative nonfiction category of the F. Scott Fitzgerald writing competition sponsored by the University of Baltimore in 2010.

SYLVIA RIOJAS VAUGHN (I'm Gatsby): I like the scene in Chapter III where Nick Carraway first meets Jay Gatsby. Nick's been invited, and no one is invited to Gatsby's parties; flappers and swells are drawn as moths to a flame. This particular page lacks lush adjectives and nouns that spark the imagination, so I wanted to see what poem hid in the text. What I found was Gatsby's smile, a bit unnerving, hiding a secret. I pictured Gatsby as Lewis Carroll's Cheshire Cat. (Text is from P. 48, *The Great Gatsby*, F. Scott Fitzgerald, First Scribner Classic/Collier Edition 1986, Macmillan Publishing Co., New York, NY.)

MELANIE VILLINES (To Look Up and Remember): I bought a used copy of *The Great Gatsby* for a dollar at a second-hand store. The underlined words made me think of when I was a young teen, just starting to read non-Nancy Drew books, and I underlined all the words I didn't know so I could look them up later. These days, I seldom encounter a word I have to look up (not bragging—I've just spent a lot of time with dictionaries), so these underlined words made me think back to when I was a young reader starting on my adventure in books.

ALAN WALOWITZ (Great Neck Record): The poem is about an artifact from the 1920s—the Gatsby era—which I see each day on the street as I leave my house here in a small corner of Great Neck, Fitzgerald's West Egg. Though the poem was not written with Gatsby in mind, it does touch on some class issues, which are certainly addressed in the novel, and still very much alive in communities like ours.

AMY SHREIBMAN WALTER (They Slipped Briskly into an Intimacy from Which They Never Recovered): All lines, including the title, are taken from various novels by F. Scott Fitzgerald

SUSANNAH WHITE (The Magician): The poem is based on the concept that Gatsby is Great because he is an illusionist or magician—a concept reinforced by the mystery surrounding him and by him vanishing when Nick first sees him looking out to the green light. Through discussing this text with many staff and pupils at the Ladies College, I've come to appreciate the themes and depth of the novel, and my poem is designed to reflect the concept of Gatsby as both an illusionist and as a man who is destroyed by his own illusions. The poem is written using the voice of Nick, the narrator, a man who makes Gatsby "great" for his readers.

NEAL WHITMAN (We Are the Lengthening Days: A Hospice Haibun): Haiku is an ancient Japanese form of poetry that has been re-formatted in English into three-lines. Though some Western poets aim to emulate the Japanese haiku of 17 sound units by writing 17 syllables, sound units are not syllables and syllables are not sound units! What is key to the haiku tradition is to be concise. What I offer is a combination of short prose and haiku, an old Japanese form known as haibun. The haiku are not meant to re-tell the prose section, but instead should create a resonance. I "found" the haiku, that is, I used the words written by Fitzgerald in Chapter IX to juxtapose poetry with prose.

ABOUT THE AUTHORS

KATIE ALIFERIS is a Greek-American poet and writer from San Francisco, California. Her poetry has been featured in *Φωνές*, *sPARKLE & bLINK*, *Unbroken* (forthcoming), *Visual Verse*, and other literary anthologies, journals, and websites. Her favorite poems are Jane Hirshfield's "The Lost Love Poems of Sappho" and C.P. Cavafy's "Όταν Διεγείρονται" ("When Roused"). When not writing, Katie can be found reading, traveling, sipping mint tea, and enjoying time with friends and family. Find Katie online via Twitter (@KatieA_SF) and at katiealferis.com.

E. KRISTIN ANDERSON is a Pushcart-nominated poet and author who grew up in Westbrook, Maine, and is a graduate of Connecticut College. She has a fancy diploma that says "B.A. in Classics," which makes her sound smart but has not helped her get any jobs in Ancient Rome. Kristin is the co-editor of *Dear Teen Me*, an anthology based on the popular website. Her poetry has been published worldwide in many magazines and anthologies and she is the author of four chapbooks: *A Jab of Deep Urgency* (Finishing Line Press) and *A Guide for the Practical Abductee* (Red Bird Chapbooks) *Pray Pray Pray: Poems I wrote to Prince in the middle of the night* (forthcoming from Porkbelly Press), and *Acoustic Battery Life* (forthcoming from ELJ Publications). She is an online editor at *Hunger Mountain* and a poetry editor at *Found Poetry Review*. Once upon a time she worked at *The New Yorker*. She now lives in Austin, Texas, where she is currently working on a full-length collection of erasure poems from women's and teen magazines. She blogs at EKristinAnderson.com.

MARIA IVANA TREVISANI BACH is a biologist, researcher, teacher, councilor of the Beigua Park, writer (animals, nature, ecology, and the battle against pollution are the themes of her literary works). She endorses the Ecopoetry Movement whose "Italian Manifesto" she wrote in 2005. The author's work includes scientific and literary articles, an Ecopoetry book (Ed. Serarcangeli Roma), and books on animals (Ed. Mursia, Milano). *The Feline Comedy by Mozot* is her last book and was presented at the Ecocriticism Congress in *Worchester University* (G.B.), in the *University* (UFPB) Joao Pessoa (Brazil), and in 2014 in the *University Castellae* (Valladolid, Spain).

JOHANNES S.H. BJERG was born in 1957. He is a Dane writing simultaneously in Danish and English. Mainly he writes (hai)ku and related forms.

JULIE E. BLOEMEKE's poetry manuscript was selected as a semifinalist in the 2014 Crab Orchard Poetry Series First Book Award and a semifinalist for the 2015 Washington Prize through Word Works. A graduate of the Bennington Writing Seminars and a 2014 fellow at the Virginia Center for the Creative Arts, her work has appeared or is forthcoming in various publications including *Gulf Coast, Chautauqua Literary Journal, Drunken Boat, Poet Lore,* and *The Southern Poetry Anthology: Georgia.* Recently, her ekphrastic work on Philip C. Curtis was selected for a limited edition chapbook anthology collaboration between the Phoenix Museum of Art and Four Chambers Press. In May 2015, she also won the 2015 ekphrastic poetry competition at the Toledo Museum of Art, where her work will be on view with the Claude Monet collection until November.

KAREN BOISSONNEAULT-GAUTHIER is a visual artist, photographer, writer, and poet. Finding the beautiful within the mundane is a joy for her. She has shot cover art for *Vine Leaves Literary Journal, Crack the Spine,* and *Zen Dixie.* Karen has also been featured in *Artemis Journal, Connotation Press, The Sonder Review, The Tishman Review, Cactus Heart Press, Synaesthesia, Dactyl, Fine Flu Literary Journal, The Scarborough Big Art Book, Sand Canyon Review, The Notebook, Shadows and Light Anthology, Vagabonds,* and *Calliope Magazine,* to name a few of the creative places she dwells. Follow Karen @KBG_Tweets and find her visual art at kcbgphoto.com.

ED BREMSON is an award-winning haiku poet who mainly builds his chapbooks from haiku and/or tanka. In 2014, a collection of his poems was published in Taiwan, and he edited a collection of Mongolian haiku published in Mongolia. His individual poems have been published in various journals. Found poetry is his real love, though, and he has a chapbook of found poems—*Like a Summer Night*—that will be released in summer 2015 by Finishing Line Press. He lives in Raleigh, North Carolina.

TANYA BRYAN is a Canadian writer with work published in *Feathertale Review, NY_____,* and *Drunk Monkeys.* She loves to travel, as well as write and draw her experiences, which are often surreal and wonderful. She can be found @tanyabryan on Twitter.

ANA MARIA CABALLERO won Colombia's José Manuel Arango National Poetry Prize in 2014 for her book *Entre domingo y domingo (From Sunday to Sunday).* Her work has appeared in over twenty publications, including *Jai-Alai, Smoking Glue Gun Magazine, Red Savina Review, Big River Poetry Review* and *CutBank.* It is forthcoming on *The Potomac* and others. Every week, she writes about poetry for *Zeteo Journal.* Her poems and book thoughts can be read at the drugstorenotebook.co.

SAM CHA received his MFA from UMass Boston in 2013, where he was the 2011 and 2012 recipient of the Academy of American Poets Award. His work has appeared (or is forthcoming from) *apt, Better, Cleaver, decomP, Memorious, Printer's Devil Review,* and a few other places. Poetry editor at *Radius,* he lives and writes in Cambridge, Massachusetts.

JAN CHRONISTER teaches English and Creative Writing at a tribal college in Minnesota. She lives in the woods near Maple, Wisconsin, where she reads and gardens when not tending students. Her chapbook *Target Practice* was published in 2009 by Parallel Press (University of Wisconsin).

MARYANN CORBETT is the author of three full-length books of poetry and two chapbooks. Her newest book *Mid Evil* is the winner of the Richard Wilbur Award, published by The University of Evansville Press. Her poems, essays, and translations appear widely in print and online journals and an assortment of anthologies. She is a past winner of the Lyric Memorial Award and the Willis Barnstone Translation Prize. She lives in Saint Paul, Minnesota, and works for the Minnesota Legislature. Her web page is maryanncorbett.com.

ANTHONY COSTELLO's poems have appeared most recently in *The Shop, Orbis, English Chicago Review, Acumen,* and *Ink, Sweat and Tears. The poems of Alain-Fournier,* a collaboration with Anita Marsh and Anthony Howell, will be published by Anvil in 2015. Lapwing Publications, Belfast, published *the Mask,* his first collection of poems, in fall 2014.

TASHA COTTER is the author of *Some Churches* (Gold Wake Press, 2013) and *That Bird Your Heart* (Finishing Line Press, 2013). Twice nominated for the Pushcart Prize, her work has appeared in journals such as *Contrary Magazine, NANO fiction,* and *Booth.* In 2015, she was named runner-up in the Carnegie Center's Next Great Writer contest. She lives in Lexington, Kentucky, where she works in higher education.

HELEN DALLAS recently commenced her BA in English Literature at the University of Cambridge. Despite being only nineteen, she takes her writing very seriously and recently had a play long-listed by the National Theatre in their New Views Playwriting Competition and a piece short-listed in the Fylde Brighter Writers' flash fiction competition.

TRACY DAVIDSON lives in Warwickshire, England, and enjoys writing poetry and flash fiction. Her work has appeared in various publications and anthologies, including *Modern Haiku, Atlas Poetica, Mslexia, The Binnacle, A Hundred Gourds, Frogpond, The Heron's Nest, Ekphrastia Gone Wild,* and *Journey to Crone.*

SUSAN DE SOLA is an American poet living in Amsterdam. Her poems have appeared in *The Hudson Review, The Hopkins Review, Ambit, River Styx,* and many other venues. She holds a PhD in English from The Johns Hopkins University and publishes scholarly essays and reviews as Susan de Sola Rodstein. She is a David Reid Poetry Translation Prize winner, and Morton Marr Poetry Prize finalist. She has published a photographic chapbook, *Little Blue Man*, from Seabiscuit Press. Find her photography at thunderbirdman.tumblr.com.

ANDREA JANELLE DICKENS currently lives in Mesa, Arizona, and teaches in the Writing Programs at Arizona State. She has had poetry published recently in Silver Birch Press' *Noir Anthology*, in *New South*, *streetcake*, *Thin Air*, *Caesura*, and *Of Zoos*. In her spare time, she is a beekeeper, a desert landscaper, and a potter.

MICHELLE DONFRIO works in the famous Leo Burnett building in Chicago and is often inspired by the cityscape. She has been published in *Poydra's Review*, *Nolos*, and has guest blogged on sites such as veganbeautyreview.com. Her motto: Art is life, and life is beauty.

JENNIFER FINSTROM teaches in the First-Year Writing Program, tutors in writing, and facilitates a writing group, Writers Guild, at DePaul University. She has been the poetry editor of *Eclectica Magazine* since October 2005, and recent publications include *Escape Into Life*, *NEAT*, *Midwestern Gothic*, and *YEW Journal*, among others. She also has work forthcoming in the Silver Birch Press *Alice in Wonderland Anthology*.

ASHLEY FORD is a poet, writer & artist who lives in Norfolk, UK, with her wife, her cat, and their three dogs. She spends her free time reading philosophy, crime novels, and psychological thrillers. She's a qualified bookkeeper and a terrible dancer. Her website can be viewed at www.ashleycaeraeonford.blogspot.com.

JEANNINE HALL GAILEY recently served as the second Poet Laureate of Redmond, Washington. She is the author of four books of poetry: *Becoming the Villainess*, *She Returns to the Floating World*, *Unexplained Fevers*, and *The Robot Scientist's Daughter*. Her website is webbish6.com.

SHIVAPRIYA GANAPATHY is from Kanchipuram, India. She graduated with a Masters degree in English Literature from Madras Christian College, and is now a research scholar, working on lesbian feminism and language. She is also an aspiring poet who experiments with new forms like micropoetry and erasure. Some of her poems have been published in *Whispers*, *Verse Wrights*, *Word Couch*, *Wordweavers*, Spilt Ink Poetry, *Sonic Boom*, and *The Squire: 1,000 Paper Cranes Anthology*. She also maintains a personal poetry blog and finds writing, therapeutic.

MARIELLE GAUTHIER is a poet and photographer living in Canada.

TRINA GAYNON has poems in the anthologies *Saint Peter's B-list: Contemporary Poems Inspired by the Saints*, *Obsession: Sestinas for the 21st*

Century, A Ritual to Read Together: Poems in Conversation with William Stafford, Phoenix Rising from the Ashes: Anthology of Sonnets of the Early Third Millennium, Bombshells and *Knocking at the Door*, as well as numerous journals including *Natural Bridge, Reed* and the final issue of *Runes*. Her chapbook *An Alphabet of Romance* is available from Finishing Line Press. Visit her at tdgaynon.webs.com.

GARY GLAUBER is a poet, fiction writer, and teacher. In April 2015, he took part in *Found Poetry Review*'s PoMoSco project. Recent poems are published or forthcoming in *Blue Heron Review, Pilgrimage Magazine, West Trade Review, Calliope Magazine, The Bookends Review, Deep Water Literary Journal, Typoetic.us, The Legendary, Xanadu,* and *Think Journal.* His first collection, *Small Consolations,* will arrive in Summer 2015 from The Aldrich Press. A chapbook entitled *Memory Marries Desire* will be available from Finishing Line Press in fall 2015.

DOUGLAS GOETSCH is the author of three books of poems, most recently *Nameless Boy* (Orchises Press, 2015), and four prizewinning chapbooks. His work has appeared numerous magazines and anthologies, including *The New Yorker, The American Scholar* and *Best American Poetry.* He is a recipient of a National Foundation for the Arts Poetry Fellowship and a Pushcart Prize, and is founding editor of Jane Street Press in New York City. Find him at www.douglasgoetsch.com.

LOIS MARIE HARROD's thirteenth and fourteenth poetry collections, *Fragments from the Biography of Nemesis* (Cherry Grove Press) and the chapbook *How Marlene Mae Longs for Truth* (Dancing Girl Press) appeared in 2013. *The Only Is* won the 2012 Tennessee Chapbook Contest (Poems & Plays), and *Brief Term,* a collection of poems about teachers and teaching, was published by Black Buzzard Press in 2011. *Cosmogony* won the 2010 Hazel Lipa Chapbook (Iowa State). She is widely published in literary journals and online ezines from *American Poetry Review* to *Zone 3.* She teaches Creative Writing at The College of New Jersey. Read her work at loismarieharrod.org.

SENNA HEYATAWIN, poet, was born in San Francisco, California, and is an enrolled member of the Choctaw Nation of Oklahoma. Her poems have been published in journals, magazines, and anthologies, and have won poetry prizes since the 1980s. She received her MFA in creative writing from San Francisco State University.

JOANIE HIEGER FRITZ ZOSIKE is a writer, actor, director, and singer splitting time between Manhattan and Manchester, New Jersey. Her work appears in the Silver Birch Press *Summer Anthology* and *Noir Erasure Poetry Anthology.* Her poems and photos appear in Three Room Press's *Maintenant* Issues 5-9. Other publications include *At the Edge*

Vol. 3 and Vol. 4, clockwise.wordpress.com and crocknbunk.com, *Flute, Helicon 9, Heresies, International Worker, Jewish Daily Forward, Levure Literraire No. 7* (online), *Life and Taxes, Nessuno Tocchi Caino, NYArts* magazine, *Public Illumination Magazine* (PIM), *Run to the Roadhouse, Nellie* online, *Womannews* and *Zeitriss.* Her work is anthologized in *Have a NYC* Vol. 3 (Ed. Peter Carlaftes, Three Rooms Press), *Between Ourselves: Letters Between Mothers and Daughters,* (Ed. Karen Payne, Mariner Publications) and *Women in American Theatre* (Eds. Helen Krich Chinoy and Linda Walsh Jenkins, TCG Publications). She is completing a book of poetry, *An Alphabet of Love,* for Barncott Press (2015). Joanie is a member of the legendary Living Theatre, director of and actor with DADAnewyork, and co-founder and co-director of *Action Racket Theatre.* She is a member of Theaters Against War (THAW), NYC Peoples Life Fund, and War Resisters League.

SHAWN P. HOSKING is a machinist by trade who dabbles in poetry.

VERONICA HOSKING is a wife, mother and poet. She lives in the desert southwest with her husband (Shawn P. Hosking, who also appears in this anthology) and two daughters. Her family and day job, cleaning the house, serve as inspiration for most of her poetry. She was the poetry editor for *MaMaZina* magazine 2006-2011. "Spikier Spongier" appeared in *Stone Crowns* magazine November 2013. "Desperate Poet" was posted on the Narrator International website and reprinted in *Poetry Nook* February 2014. "Rain Drops" was published in *Half New Year Poetry Collection* (Silver Birch Press, 2014). Veronica keeps a poetry blog at vhosking.wordpress.com.

MATHIAS JANSSON is a Swedish art critic and poet. He has contributed with visual poetry to magazines such as *Lex-ICON, Anatematiskpress, Quarter After #4,* and *Maintenant 8: A Journal of Contemporary Dada.* He has also published a chapbook at this is visual poetry and contributed with erasure poetry to anthologies from Silver Birch Press. Visit him at mathiasjansson72.blogspot.se.

JEN CULLERTON JOHNSON has an MFA from the University of New Orleans. Her essays have been published in various literary magazines. She is the author of *Seeds of Change,* a children's book and a textbook called *Green Literacy: Fueling Critical Conversations.* Currently, she lives in Chicago and teaches at the largest juvenile detention center in the country.

DAVID M. KATZ is the author of three books of poems: *Stanzas on Oz, Poems 2011-2014* (Dos Madres Press), *Claims of Home, Poems 1984-2010* (Dos Madres Press), and *The Warrior in the Forest* (House of Keys Press). His poems have appeared in *Poetry, The New Criterion, The Paris Review, PN Review, The Raintown Review, Alabama Literary Review,* and

Southwest Review. He lives in New York City, where he works as a financial journalist.

BECCA KLAVER is the author of the poetry collection *LA Liminal* (Kore Press, 2010) and several chapbooks, including *Nonstop Pop* (Bloof Books, 2013) and *Merrily, Merrily* (Lame House Press, 2013). A graduate of the University of Southern California and Columbia College Chicago, she is currently a PhD candidate in English at Rutgers University, where she's writing a dissertation on late-20th-century women's poetry, feminism, and the everyday. Becca grew up in Milwaukee, Wisconsin, and now lives in Brooklyn, New York, where she hosts the What's So Hot salon series.

LAURIE KOLP, author of *Upon the Blue Couch* (Winter Goose Publishing, 2014) and *Hello It's Your Mother* (Finishing Line Press, October 2015) serves as president of Texas Gulf Coast Writers and each month gathers with local members of the Poetry Society of Texas. Laurie's poems have appeared in numerous print and online journals worldwide including the *2015 Poet's Market, Scissors & Spackle, North Dakota Quarterly, Blue Fifth Review*, and *Pirene's Fountain*. Find out more at her website, lauriekolp.com.

LINDA KRAUS has taught English and Film Studies at the college and university levels. She has written film criticism, short fiction, and poetry since adolescence and has published both poetry and film criticism.

JEAN L. KREILING is the author of the recently published collection *The Truth in Dissonance* (Kelsay Books, 2014). Her work has appeared widely in print and online journals, including *American Arts Quarterly, Angle, The Evansville Review, Measure*, and *Mezzo Cammin*, as well as in several anthologies. She is a past winner of the String Poet Prize and the Able Muse Write Prize, and has been a finalist for the Frost Farm Prize, the Howard Nemerov Sonnet Award, and the Richard Wilbur Poetry Award.

KATHRYN KULPA fell in love with *The Great Gatsby* in ninth grade and proceeded to read everything by Fitzgerald she could find. She is the author of the award-winning short story collection *Pleasant Drugs* (Mid-List Press) and has published fiction in *Hayden's Ferry Review, Monkeybicycle, NANO Fiction*, and *Smokelong Quarterly*. Her short story "Lights Out: Zelda at Highland Hospital," inspired by Zelda Fitzgerald, was featured in the anthology *Up, Do Flash Fiction by Women Writers*. Find her on Twitter @KathrynKulpa or at kathrynkulpa.com.

DAVID W. LANDRUM teaches Literature at Grand Valley State University in Allendale, Michigan. His poetry has appeared widely.

SAMANTHA LEVAN is a poet, novelist, lecturer, and researcher for Christopher Newport University and Old Dominion University in Hampton Roads, Virginia. She received her Master of Arts in Lifespan and Digital Communication from Old Dominion University in 2013. Her social science research focuses on the dark side of communication (i.e., infidelity, aggression, addiction) and differing relational rules in alternative interpersonal relationships. She is currently finishing her first Southern Literature novel *The Oak Tree* and her first poetry book *Underneath the Mimosa*.

STEFANIE LIPSEY is a poet and public school librarian/teacher in Gatsby country on Long Island. Her work has been published in anthologies and journals including *Southword, Long Island Quarterly, Big City Lit*, and *Halfway Down the Stairs*. She has facilitated writing workshops at Hofstra University, The Omega Institute, and at libraries and retreat centers. Stefanie holds an MFA in Creative Writing from Queens College, CUNY.

LYNLEYSHIMAT LYS is back in Brooklyn after five years in Jerusalem, and studies in the MFA program in Creative Writing and Literary Translation at Queens College-CUNY. Recent readings include the Lamprophonic and Dead Rabbits Reading Series in New York and at the Massachusetts Poetry Festival. Lynley also held a residency at the Louis Armstrong Archive at Queens College, and will be teaching Creative Writing at Queens in fall 2015. Visit the author online at lynleyshimatlyspoetry.weebly.com.

CAOLAN MADDEN lives in Brooklyn with her husband and daughter. She is a PhD candidate in English literature at Rutgers University, where she teaches literature, creative writing, and composition, and is working on a dissertation on Victorian and modernist women poets. She has an MFA in poetry from Johns Hopkins University; her work has appeared in *Triple Canopy, Bone Bouquet, Iron Horse Literary Review,* and *Gritty Silk. Girl Talk Triptych,* a play she wrote in collaboration with other members of the poetry collective (G)IRL, was performed at Small Press Traffic's 2015 Poets Theater, and contains multiple Gatsby references. Caolan is also a regular contributor to the feminist pop-culture blog WEIRD SISTER.

SHAHÉ MANKERIAN's manuscript, *History of Forgetfulness,* has been a finalist at four prestigious competitions: the 2013 Crab Orchard Series in Poetry Open Competition, the 2013 Bibby First Book Competition, the Quercus Review Press, Fall Poetry Book Award (2013), and the 2014 White Pine Press Poetry Prize. Shahé serves as the principal of St. Gregory Hovsepian School in Pasadena and co-directs the Los Angeles Writing Project. He has been honored with the Los Angeles Music Center's BRAVO Award, which recognizes teachers for innovation and excellence in arts education.

MARJORIE MANWARING, a freelance writer/editor living in Seattle, is an editorial board member for Floating Bridge Press (floatingbridgepress.org), a publisher and promoter of Washington State poets. Her poems have appeared in a variety of journals and anthologies, including *Crab Creek Review* and *A Face to Meet the Faces: An Anthology of Contemporary Persona Poetry*, and have been featured on Seattle's National Public Radio affiliate KUOW. Her first full-length collection, *Search for a Velvet-Lined Cape* (Mayapple Press), was released in January 2013. Visit her at mmanwaring.com.

JOHN MCCARTHY is the author of the forthcoming collection *Ghost County* (MG Press, 2016). His poems have appeared in *The Pinch, The Minnesota Review, Redivider, Salamander, RHINO*, and *Jabberwock Review*. He is the Managing Editor of *Quiddity* International Literary Journal and Public-Radio Program.

CATFISH MCDARIS's most infamous chapbook is *Prying* with Jack Micheline and Charles Bukowski. He's done over twenty chaps in the last twenty-five years. He is an aging New Mexican living near Milwaukee. He has four walls, a ceiling, heat, food, a woman, a daughter, two cats, a typing machine, and a mailbox.

GEORGE MCKIM has an MFA in Painting. His poetry has appeared or is forthcoming in *Dear Sirs, Shampoo, Diagram, elimae, Ditch, Cricket Online Review, Blaze Vox, The Found Poetry Review* Pulitzer Remix Project, and others. His chapbook *Found & Lost* is forthcoming from Silver Birch Press in 2015.

SARAH FAWN MONTGOMERY holds an MFA in creative nonfiction from California State University-Fresno and a PhD in creative writing from the University of Nebraska-Lincoln, where she teaches and works as *Prairie Schooner*'s Nonfiction Assistant Editor. She is the author of *The Astronaut Checks His Watch* (Finishing Line Press). Her work has been listed as notable several times in *Best American Essays*, and her poetry and prose have appeared in various magazines including *Confrontation, Crab Orchard Review, DIAGRAM, Fugue, Georgetown Review, The Los Angeles Review, North Dakota Quarterly, The Pinch, Puerto del Sol, Southeast Review, Zone 3*, and others.

CHRISTINA MURPHY's poetry is an exploration of consciousness as subjective experience, and her poems appear in a wide range of journals and anthologies, including, in *PANK, La Fovea, Pear Noir!*, and *Hermeneutic Chaos Literary Journal*, and in the anthologies *Let the Sea Find its Edges*, edited by the distinguished Australian poet, Michael Fitzgerald-Clarke, and in *Remaking Moby-Dick*, edited by Trish Harris and published by EU Art Line. Her work has been nominated multiple times for the Pushcart Prize and for the Best of the Net Anthology.

LESLIE NICHOLS is an artist who uses a variety of found and original text to create images. Her most well-known works are created on manual typewriters and featured in *Typewriter Art: A Modern Anthology*. Her work is in permanent collections including the Sackner Archive of Concrete and Visual Poetry. She lives and works in Kentucky.

LEWIS OAKWOOD has been a Thought Researcher for the past fifteen years. The exploration of the origins/nature of thought has taken him to Oregon (USA), Pune (India), Khangai Mountains (Mongolia), Mount Athos (Greece), and Troodos Mountains (Cyprus). An experimental poetry hobbyist, he has spent quite a few years inquiring into the "natural state" (U.G. Krishnamurti) and the ideas/teachings of Chandra Mohan Jain. He is currently living in West Sussex, U.K

ALYSSON B. PARKER is a poet by passion but a high school English teacher by financial necessity. She was a first-prize winner for poetry in *The Binnacle* (2014) and was nominated for the Pushcart Prize. In addition, she has published in *Narrative Northeast*; *Postcards, Poems and Prose*; *Northern New England Review*; *Ophelia Street*; *Deep South* (New Zealand), *The Dominion Review, A Room of Her Own, ExPat Lit*, and other publications. Former senior editor and review writer for *En Pointe Magazine*, Alysson has lived in many different countries and a variety of funky situations, but right now she and her family—plus two cats and a mutt who should be paying rent—live just outside of Boston.

MARTHA PATTERSON is the author of more than one hundred plays and has been published in four anthologies by the International Centre for Women Playwrights as well as in collections by Pioneer Drama Service, Smith & Kraus/Applause Books, and JAC Publishing. Her work has been produced Off-Off-Broadway (Harold Clurman Theatre) and in eighteen states, as well as in England (Bread & Roses Theatre), Scotland (Quids in Theatre), Denmark (Belarusian Dream Theatre), Korea (Seoul Players), and Australia (Short+Sweet Festival). She earned her B.A. from Mount Holyoke College and an M.A. from Emerson College, both degrees in Theatre. She lives in Boston, Massachusetts. Her website is mpatterson125933.wix.com/Martha-patterson-

JAMES PENHA, a native New Yorker, has lived for the past twenty years in Indonesia. He has been nominated for Pushcart Prizes in fiction and in poetry. *Snakes and Angels*, a collection of his adaptations of classic Indonesian folk tales, won the 2009 Cervena Barva Press fiction chapbook contest; *No Bones to Carry*, a volume of his poetry, earned the 2007 New Sins Press Editors' Choice Award. Penha edits *The New Verse News*, an online journal of current-events poetry.

DAVID S. POINTER's work appears in the *Bukowski Anthology* (Silver Birch Press, 2013). His newest poetry book is entitled *Beyond Shark Tag Bay* sold online at Blurb Books (blurb.com).

CHRISTINA M. RAU is the author of the poetry chapbooks *Wake-BreatheMove* (Finishing Line Press, 2015) and *For The Girls, I* (Dancing Girl Press, 2014). The founder of Poets In Nassau, a reading circuit on Long Island, New York, she teaches at Nassau Community College, where she also edits *The Nassau Review*. Her poetry has appeared on gallery walls in The Ekphrastic Poster Show, on car magnets for The Living Poetry Project, and most recently in the journals *Crony*, *Redheaded Stepchild*, and *The Main Street Rag*. In her non-writing life, she occasionally practices yoga and line dances on other occasions. Find her links on alifeofwe.blogspot.com.

SUZANNE RAWLINSON currently works in a school as a teaching assistant. She has been writing short stories of various genres and small poetry pieces since completing her studies in Creative Writing. She is currently working on a novel related to family life and a script for a TV/Radio drama. In 2013 she had a piece of poetry published in an online magazine. She enjoys writing truthfully about real life experiences that people can relate to.

PATRICK T. REARDON is a Chicagoan, born and bred. He has written five books, has published essays and poems widely, and is writing a book about the elevated railroad Loop in Chicago. Follow him on his blog at patricktreardon.com.

MARYBETH RUA-LARSEN lives on the south coast of Massachusetts and teaches at Bristol Community College. Her poems, essays, flash fiction, and reviews have appeared or are forthcoming in *American Arts Quarterly*, *The Raintown Review*, *Cleaver*, *Measure*, *Literary Orphans*, and *Unsplendid*, among others. She won the 2011 Over the Edge New Writer of the Year Competition in Poetry in Galway, Ireland, and her chapbook *Nothing In-Between* was published by Barefoot Muse Press.

SHLOKA SHANKAR is a freelance writer from Bangalore, India. A wordsmith by craft, she loves experimenting with different kinds of found poetry techniques. Some of her erasures have appeared in *Ofi Press Mexico*, *Literary Orphans*, *Poetry WTF?!*, *Otoliths*, *The Gambler Mag*, *Straight Forward Poetry*, and other publications. She is also the founding editor of the literary & arts journal *Sonic Boom*.

SHEIKHA A. currently lives in Karachi, Pakistan, after moving there from the United Arab Emirates, and believes the transition has definitely stimulated a different tunnel of thought. With publication credits in magazines such as *Red Fez*, *American Diversity Report*, *Open Road Review*, *Mad Swirl*, *Danse Macabre du Jour*, *Rose Red Review*, *The Penmen*

Review, among many others, as well as several anthologies, she has also authored a poetry collection entitled *Spaced,* published by Hammer and Anvil Books, available on Kindle. She edits poetry for eFiction India. Visit her blog at sheikha82.wordpress.com.

EDWARD W.L. SMITH, living part-time on a small barrier island reckons with multiple muses, writing poetry and mystery, essays and nonfiction books, painting and playing tenor saxophone. Therein, he seeks balance of logos and eros. His most recent book is *The Psychology of Artists and the Arts* (McFarland, 2012). He is an Emeritus Professor of Psychology, Georgia Southern University.

MATTHEW OLDHAM SMITH is a screenwriter, blogger, and urban planner. He has written several feature film screenplays and television dramas, independently and with long-time friend Marianne Titiriga, including the selection from *The Roaring Twenties* included in this anthology. Matthew resides with his husband and young son in the historic seaside city of Salem, Massachusetts.

SHERRY STEINER lives in Housatonic, Massachusetts, and is originally from New York City. She is a published writer of off-beat poetry, monologues, flash fiction, and musical performance pieces, and is an arts educator, exhibiting visual artist, and more. Visit her at sherrysteiner.com

CHRISTINE STROUD is originally from eastern North Carolina, but currently lives in Pittsburgh and works as the Senior Editor for Autumn House Press. She has an MFA in Creative Writing from Chatham University. Her chapbook, *The Buried Return,* was released by Finishing Line Press in March 2014.

MARIANNE TITIRIGA is a screenwriter/producer born and raised in Torrance, California. Since age eleven, Marianne has known that she wanted to create "Movie Magic," and with the inspirational influence of her parents, Andrew and Elizabeth Titiriga, she was able to make her childhood dreams a reality. Presently, she independently writes both animated and live action films. The selection in this anthology was taken from *The Roaring Twenties,* a screenplay she co-wrote with longtime friend, Matthew Oldham Smith. Marianne resides in Los Angeles, California, and is currently the creator and executive producer of an animated feature under 20th Century Fox.

SALLY TONER lives in the suburbs of Washington D.C. with her husband and two teen daughters. A high school English teacher of over twenty years, her fiction has appeared in *Gargoyle Magazine* and *Defying Gravity*—a collection of work from D.C.-area women writers. Her poetry is forthcoming in *Clementine* poetry journal and *The Delmarva Review.*

LEE UPTON is the author of six books of poetry including *Undid in the Land of Undone, Civilian Histories*, and *Approximate Darling*; the story collection *The Tao of Humiliation*; the essay collection *Swallowing the Sea: ON Writing & Ambition, Boredom, Purity & Secrecy*; the novella *The Guide to the Flying Island*; and several books of critical prose, most recently *Defensive Measures: The Poetry of Niedecker, Bishop, Glück, and Carson*. She is a professor of English and the writer-in-residence at Lafayette College. *Bottle the Bottles the Bottles the Bottles* is the winner of the 2014 Cleveland State University Poetry Center Open Book Competition, selected by Erin Belieu.

SYLVIA RIOJAS VAUGHN has poems in *Dialogo*, a publication of DePaul University, and *Desde Hong Kong: Poets in Conversation with Octavio Paz*. Her work has appeared in *Red River Review*, and the anthologies *Elegant Rage: A Poetic Tribute to Woody Guthrie*, and *Bridge of Fates*, a 2014 Lost Tower Publication. She took first place in the Richardson Public Library poetry contest, and has placed in Ohio Poetry Day competitions. Her play, *La Tamalada*, was produced in Fort Worth. She is a member of Dallas Poets Community.

MELANIE VILLINES is a writer, editor, researcher, and publisher who lives in Los Angeles. Her comic crime novel *Windy City Sinners* will appear in fall 2015 from Sugar Skull Press.

RACHEL VOSS is a high school English teacher (who teaches *Gatsby* to her juniors) living in Queens, New York. She graduated with a degree in creative writing and literature from SUNY Purchase College. Her work has previously appeared in *Hanging Loose Magazine*, *Blast Furnace*, *Newtown Literary*, and *The New Verse News*, among others, and is forthcoming in *Unsplendid*.

ALAN WALOWITZ has been writing poems for many years, and currently on Long Island, where he keeps his eye on his native borough of Queens from his front door. Some days he teaches at Manhattanville College in Purchase, New York, a little to the north, and on other days at St. John's University, a bit to the west.

AMY SCHREIBMAN WALTER is an American poet living in London. A recent Visiting Writer at The American Academy of Rome, Amy's poems have appeared in numerous publications on either side of the Atlantic. She is the co-editor of *here/there:poetry*.

SUSANNAH WHITE is a qualified teacher with an M.A in Creative Writing from King Alfred's College in Winchester, United Kingdom. Susannah has taught at a number of independent secondary schools including the famous Cheltenham Ladies College, where *The Great Gatsby* was studied as part of the IGCSE syllabus. She is now based at the University of Gloucestershire, where she supports students in a number of disciplines including creative writing.

LIN WHITEHOUSE has a BA Hons degree in Creative Writing. Her passion is playwriting, and she has had several short plays performed in theatres across the North of England. A published poet and short story writer, she is currently writing a novel.

NEAL WHITMAN lives with his wife, Elaine, in Pacific Grove, California. They both volunteer for The Hospice of the Central Coast for which Elaine plays the Native American flute and Neal is a bereavement counselor. The Whitmans also combine his poetry and her Native American flute in public recitals. Neal teaches a workshop, "Haiku for Everyone, for Anyone," to raise funds for not-for-profit organizations and is the haiku editor for *Pulse: Voices from the Heart of Medicine* (pulsevoices.org).

SCOTT WIGGERMAN is the author of three books of poetry, *Leaf and Beak: Sonnets, Presence*, and *Vegetables and Other Relationships*; and the editor of several volumes, including *Wingbeats: Exercises & Practice in Poetry, Lifting the Sky: Southwestern Haiku & Haiga*, and *Wingbeats II*. Recent poems have appeared in *Decades Review, Frogpond, Pinyon Review, Borderlands: Texas Poetry Review*, and the anthologies *This Assignment Is So Gay, Pushing the Envelope*, and *The Queer South*. He is chief editor for Dos Gatos Press, now of Albuquerque, New Mexico.

MATTHEW WILSON'S writing has appeared in over one hundred and fifty places, including as *Horror Zine, Star Line, Spellbound, Illumen, Apokrupha Press, Hazardous Press, Gaslight Press, Sorcerers Signal*, and many more. He is currently editing his first novel and can be contacted on twitter @matthew94544267.

THEODORA ZIOLKOWSKI'S poems and short stories have appeared or are forthcoming in *Prairie Schooner, Short Fiction (England)*, and *Gargoyle Magazine*, among other journals, anthologies, and exhibits. She lives in Tuscaloosa, Alabama, and is originally from Easton, Pennsylvania.

ACKNOWLEDGMENTS

"Oh, Zelda" by Ana Maria Caballero was originally published by *East Coast Ink Magazine*.

"To the Statue of F. Scott Fitzgerald in Rice Park, Seen from the 53B" by Maryann Corbett was first published in *Verse Wisconsin* (Fall 2010) and reprinted in the collection *Breath Control* (David Robert Books, 2012).

"Heroines at 40: Daisy Buchanan" by Jeannine Hall Gailey previously appeared in *Ragazine*, 2015.

"I am not even faintly like a rose" by Gary Glauber was first published online at *Verbatim Poetry*.

"Swimming to New Zealand" by Douglas Goetsch, originally appeared in *Plume* online, and subsequently in *Nameless Boy* (Orchises Press, 2015) and *The Plume Anthology of Poetry*, Vol. 3 (MadHat Press, 2015).

"The Last Page" by David M. Katz was first published in *Stanzas on Oz, Poems 2011-2014* (Dos Madres Press, 2015).

"Thinking About Someone I Used To Love" by Marjorie Manwaring was previously published in the author's collection *Search for a Velvet-lined Cape* (Mayapple Press, 2013) and in *Fire On Her Tongue: An eBook Anthology of Contemporary Women's Poetry* (Two Sylvias Press, 2013).

"Nick in Heat" by James Penha was published as "Nick Carraway Out on the Town" in *Glitterwolf* #8.

"Patience" by Sally Toner took first place in the creative nonfiction category of the F. Scott Fitzgerald writing competition sponsored by the University of Baltimore in 2010.

INDEX OF AUTHORS

David W. Landrum / 35
Samantha LeVan / 16
Stefanie Lipsey / 127
LynleyShimat Lys / 159
Caolan Madden / 36-37
Shahé Mankerian / 139
Marjorie Manwaring / 38-39
John McCarthy / 101
Catfish McDaris / 78
George McKim / 17
Sarah Fawn Montgomery / 40
Christina Murphy / 79
Leslie Nichols / 18-19
Lewis Oakwood / 102
Alysson B. Parker / 41
Martha Patterson / 80-82
James Penha / 103-105
David S. Pointer / 128
Christina M. Rau / 140-141
Suzanne Rawlinson / 160-161
Patrick T. Reardon / 84-85
Marybeth Rua-Larsen / 106
Shloka Shankar / 108-109
Sheikha A. / 42
Edward W.L. Smith / 110-113
Matthew Oldham Smith / 142-148
Sherry Steiner / 129
Christine Stroud / 86
Marianne Titiriga / 142-148
Sally Toner / 122-123
Lee Upton / 162
Sylvia Riojas Vaughn / 88-89
Melanie Villines / 163
Rachel Voss / 90
Alan Walowitz / 91
Amy Schreibman Walter / 164-165
Susannah White / 114
Lin Whitehouse / 92
Neal Whitman / 93-94
Scott Wiggerman / 95
Matthew Wilson / 149
Theodora Ziolkowski / 43

ZELDA & SCOTT FITZGERALD
DAISY BUCHANAN & JAY GATSBY

EDITOR'S NOTE: At age twenty-one, F. Scott Fitzgerald meets eighteen-year-old Zelda Sayre, the model for Gatsby's love Daisy Buchanan, in July 1918, when as a U.S. Army second lieutenant he's stationed in her hometown of Montgomery, Alabama. WWI ends before Scott takes part in the fighting, and after his release from service he asks Zelda to marry him. But within months Zelda, the golden girl daughter of a prominent family, breaks off the engagement, believing Scott, a struggling author, will not be able to support her. As pampered Southern belles, Zelda and Daisy share the belief that "rich girls don't marry poor boys." Scott determines to win back Zelda—trying his luck as an advertising writer in New York, before heading to his childhood home in St. Paul, Minnesota, where he writes his first novel, *This Side of Paradise*—published in March 1920 to critical and commercial success, and allowing him to convince Zelda to marry him the following month. *The Great Gatsby* is in some respects Fitzgerald's meditation on what would have happened if he hadn't made something of himself in time to prevent Zelda from marrying a wealthy rival.

Drawings of Zelda & F. Scott Fitzgerald by Gordon Bryan (1921).

Made in the USA
Charleston, SC
27 June 2015